Life in
IRELAND

L. M. CULLEN

B. T. Batsford Ltd   London

First published 1968
First paperback edition 1979
© L.M. Cullen

ISBN 0 7134 1449 9

Made and printed in Great Britain
by The Anchor Press Ltd, Tiptree, Essex
for the publishers
B. T. BATSFORD LTD
4 Fitzhardinge Street, London W1H 0AH

LIFE IN IRELAND

(Overleaf) An Irish country inn

Preface

In the course of selecting the illustrations for this book I have made heavy demands on the time and knowledge of many individuals. I am especially grateful to Miss M. Deignan and Mr Liam Byrne of the National Library, Dublin; Mr James White, Director, and Mr Michael Wynne of the National Gallery of Ireland; Mr Noel Nesbitt of the Ulster Museum; Mr S. O'Coigligh of the Public Museum, Cork; Dr A. T. Lucas, Director of the National Museum of Ireland; Messrs Leclerc and Bambury of the National Monuments Division, Office of Public Works, Dublin; Professor J. F. M. Lydon, Captain Kevin Danaher and Dr H. S. Corran, Guinness Museum.

Of the many secondary works consulted, I have in particular made much use of the works on Irish social or economic history by Dr E. MacLysaght, C. Maxwell and T. W. Freeman, especially on account of the contemporary evidence often quoted at length in them.

I am grateful, also, to my colleagues, Professor J. A. Otway-Ruthven, who commented on Chapter II, and Professor J. F. M. Lydon, who commented on Chapters I and II; to Mr J. H. Talbot, who read the proofs, and to my wife, who has made many comments and suggestions.

L. M. C.

Trinity College,
Dublin
June, 1968

TO MY WIFE

Contents

PREFACE		v
ACKNOWLEDGMENT		viii
LIST OF ILLUSTRATIONS		ix
I	A Rural World	1
II	Conflict in Ireland: the Old Order and the New Towns 800–1550	20
III	A Period of Change 1550–1700	50
IV	Town and Country in the Eighteenth Century	70
V	Life in the Eighteenth Century	93
VI	Rural Crisis	118
VII	Post-Famine Ireland	144
INDEX		173

Acknowledgment

The author and publishers wish to thank the following for the illustrations appearing in this book: the Board of Trinity College, Dublin for pages 8, 11, 13, 15, 36, 42, 54 and 55; the Trustees of the British Museum for pages 25 and 98; the Commissioners of Public Works, Monuments Division for pages 9, 10, 14, 17, 22, 26, 33, 40 and 57; Cork Public Museum for pages 67 and 88; Ghent University Library for page 39; the Guinness Museum for pages 85, 149, 151 and 164–5; the Irish Folklore Commission for pages 129 and 145; King's Inn Library for page 32; Dr H. A. Meek, Department of Architecture, Queen's University, Belfast for page 12; the National Gallery of Ireland for pages 78, 94, 103, 134 and 136; The National Library of Ireland for the frontispiece, and pages 24, 27, 51, 52, 56, 59, 61, 63, 65, 66, 68, 73, 86, 89, 101, 106, 108, 109, 114, 116, 120, 121, 122, 123, 127, 130–31, 133, 135, 139, 142, 147, 153, 155, 156, 158, 159, 160, 161, 167 and 171; the National Maritime Museum for page 28; the National Museum of Ireland for pages 3 and 64; Public Record Office Ireland for page 91; Mrs O'Riordain for page 7; Thomas Pakenham for page 74; Ulster Museum for pages 77, 79, 81, 83, 90, 105, 111, 113, 136, 137, 148, 163 and 168; Captain Kevin Danaher for page 157; Earl of Meath for page 71; State Archives of Pennsylvania for pages 75 and 87; Frazer and Haughton Ltd for page 82.

The author and publishers would also like to thank Messrs Routledge and Kegan Paul for permission to quote on page 109 from *The Life, Times and Music of Carolan* by D. O'Sullivan, 1958, and Longmans Green Ltd for the quotation on page 154 from *Bowen's Court* by E. Bowen, 1942.

The Illustrations

Stag caught in a trap *From a carving from the shaft of a cross from Banagher*	3
Burnt outline of hut in Grange Ring-fort	7
Man on horseback *Drawing from the Book of Kells*	8
Horsemen and chariot *Carving from a cross at Ahenny, co. Tipperary (eighth century)*	9
Foundation of Monastery of Clonmacnoise (sixth century) *From tenth-century Cross of the Scriptures at Clonmacnoise*	10
Monastic scribe at work *From the Book of Kells*	11
Cleric bearing pastoral staff and bell *Carving on stone in wall of White Island Church, Lower Lough Erne*	12
Warrior with spear and shield *From the Book of Kells*	13
Seventh-century warrior with sword and shield *Carving from a stone at Carndonagh, co. Donegal*	14
Monk with book *From the Book of Kells*	14
Harp-player *Carving from a cross at Castledermot (tenth century)*	17
Composition of a book at Kildare *Giraldus Cambrensis, Topography of Ireland, c. 1200. Reproduction in Gilbert, Facsimiles of the National Manuscripts of Ireland, Vol. II*	21
Two knights in armour *Carving from a flagstone at Jerpoint Abbey*	22
Suitors before the Court of Exchequer *From the Red Book of the Exchequer in Ireland (fifteenth century). Reproduced in Gilbert, Facsimiles of the National Manuscripts of Ireland, Vol. III*	23
Irish Kings *Drawing by Petrie of frescoes at Abbey Knockmoy, Galway. From Dublin Penny Journal, January 1833*	24
Use of the axe *From Giraldus Cambrensis, Topography of Ireland, c. 1200*	25
Irish gallowglasses or mercenaries *From a group of eight carved figures on a tomb at Roscommon Abbey (fifteenth century)*	26

THE ILLUSTRATIONS

Hill-top residence of the O'Hagans at Tullaghoge *Detail from a map by Bartlett, c. 1600* — 27

Sir John Moriz, Deputy-Governor in Ireland for Edward III, 1346 *Drawing from an illustrated Charter Roll of Waterford (close of fourteenth century). Reproduced in Gilbert, Facsimiles of the National Manuscripts of Ireland, Vol. IV* — 27

Inauguration ceremony of an Irish chieftain (O'Neill) *Detail from a map by Bartlett, c. 1600* — 28

Meeting of Art MacMorrogh, King of Leinster and the Earl of Gloucester, 1399 *Illuminated drawing in Creton, History of Richard, King of England. Reproduced in Gilbert, Facsimiles of the National Manuscripts of Ireland, Vol. III* — 29

Cattle-raid *Woodcut from John Derricke, Image of Ireland, 1581* — 30

Ploughing, digging and threshing in the fifteenth century *Drawing from a Gaelic manuscript* — 32

Fifteenth-century hunting scene *Mural painting in Holycross Abbey* — 33

Waterford in 1566 *Detail from Register Book of the City of Waterford. Reproduced in Gilbert, Facsimiles of the National Manuscripts of Ireland, Vol. IV* — 34

Monks singing Psalms *Miniature from Psalter of Cathedral of Holy Trinity, now Christ Church, Dublin. Reproduced in Gilbert, Facsimiles of the National Manuscripts of Ireland, Vol. IV* — 35

Sixteenth-century ship *Detail from sixteenth-century map* — 36

Net-fishing from a boat *Detail from a map, c. 1580. Reproduced in Gilbert, Facsimiles of the National Manuscripts of Ireland, Vol. IV* — 37

Mayor of Dublin *Drawing from an illustrated Charter Roll of Waterford (close of fourteenth century). Reproduced in Gilbert, Facsimiles of the National Manuscripts of Ireland, Vol. IV* — 38

Irish townswomen, *c.* 1575 *Water-colour by Lucas De Heere* — 39

A noblewoman, possibly the first Countess of Ormonde *Carving on a flagstone at St Mary's Church, Gowran* — 40

Tilting *Detail from seventeenth-century pictorial map of Galway* — 42

Soldiers wading into the sea to unload provisions for the relief of Richard II's army on the east coast of Ireland *Creton, History of Richard, King of England. Reproduced in Gilbert, Facsimiles of the National Manuscripts of Ireland, Vol. III* — .43

An Irish chieftain feasting *Woodcut from John Derricke, Image of Ireland, 1581* — 44

Irish chieftain in full dress *Woodcut from John Derricke, Image of Ireland, 1581* — 46

Head of an Irish chieftain, Turloch O'Neill, 1575 *Ink drawing by Barnaby Googe* — 47

THE ILLUSTRATIONS

Milking a cow *Drawing from Dingley, Observations in a Voyage through the Kingdom of Ireland, c. 1675–80*	51
Machinery of a water-mill *Drawing from Dingley, Observations in a Voyage through the Kingdom of Ireland, c. 1675–80*	52
Settlers' houses and church in co. Derry *Detail from a map (1622) of the Fishmongers Buildinge at Balle Kelle in the Survey by Thomas Phillips and Ralph Hudson. Reproduced in Gilbert, Facsimiles of the National Manuscripts of Ireland, Vol. IV*	53
Windmill outside the town of Youghal *Detail from a prospect of Youghal in Thomas Stafford, Pacata Hibernia, 1633*	53
'An Inn for Travailers' *Detail from an early seventeenth-century map*	54
A ferry carrying men and a horse across the Foyle at Derry *Detail from an early seventeenth-century map of Derry*	54
House and fort at Omagh *Detail from an early seventeenth-century map*	55
The Duke of Ormonde's house at Kilkenny from the bridge *A drawing by Francis Place, 1698–9*	56
An Irish nobleman and his wife *Effigies from a tomb at Sligo Abbey, erected 1624*	57
Stables built at Rallahine Castle, co. Clare *Drawing from Dingley, Observations in a Voyage through the Kingdom of Ireland, c. 1675–80*	59
Irish cabins outside the Fort of Monaghan *Detail from a map by Bartlett, c. 1602*	61
Village of Staplestown, co. Carlow *Drawing from Dingley, Observations in a Voyage through the Kingdom of Ireland, c. 1675–80*	63
Five men doing a sword-dance *From an engraved bone book-cover*	64
Galway in 1685 *From Phillips' Survey, 1685*	65
An ancient wooden house *Drawing from the Dublin Penny Journal, February 1833*	66
Street scene, Cork, *c.* 1630 *From 'The Irish resisting toll at Roche's Castle'. Nineteenth-century copy of a contemporary drawing*	67
A Ringsend coach *Drawing from Dingley, Observations in a Voyage through the Kingdom of Ireland, c. 1675–80*	68
Old house in Marrowbone Lane, Dublin *Drawing from the Dublin Penny Journal, February 1833*	68
The Kilruddery Hunt, co. Wicklow, *c.* 1730–40	71
Shops in Castle Street, Cork, 1796 *Detail from an aquatint*	73
An Irish road scene, *c.* 1737 *From the Journal of George Edward Pakenham, 1737–9*	74
An Irish cart *Drawing from the notebooks of Joshua Gilpin, 1796*	75

THE ILLUSTRATIONS

Turf boat on the Shannon at Limerick *Detail from an early nineteenth-century oil-painting*	77
Grand Canal Hotel, Portobello *Aquatint by James Ford*	78
Ploughing and sowing *Detail from an engraving of a drawing by William Hincks, 1783*	79
Haymaking *Detail from a water-colour by John Nixon, late eighteenth century*	81
View of Hillmount bleachgreen and house *From an oil-painting*	82
Brown linen market at Banbridge *Engraving of a drawing by William Hincks, 1783*	83
Fire-fighting in the eighteenth century *Engraving from an insurance policy issued by the Hibernian Insurance Company in 1790*	85
The walls of Derry *An early nineteenth-century engraving by Bartlett*	86
Drawing wire at a Dublin wire-mill *Drawing from the notebooks of Joshua Gilpin, 1796*	87
View of B. Sullivan's paper manufactory, ironworks and foundry, Beechmount, near Cork *Engraving, probably early nineteenth-century*	88
Cutting and packing meat for export, Cork *Detail from Survey of the City and Suburb of Cork, J. Rocque, 1773*	88
Westmoreland Street and D'Olier Street seen from Carlisle Bridge *Engraving of drawing by S. F. Brocas, 1820*	89
High Street, Belfast, 1786 *Water-colour by John Nixon*	90
Turf sales in Dublin *Drawing from a contemporary broadsheet 'The Dublin Cries'*	91
Group of eighteenth-century gentlemen *From 'The Hell-Fire Club' an oil-painting by James Worsdale, c. 1735–8*	94
View of Catholic chapel at Ardglass, co. Carlow, 1794 *Engraving from Francis Grose, Antiquities of Ireland, 1795*	95
The country schoolmaster *Oil-painting by Nathaniel Grogan*	98
Turnip, a celebrated gelding *From an aquatint*	101
Members of the family of Richard Lovell Edgeworth, including his daughter, Maria *A crayon drawing by Adam Buck, 1787*	103
Harp Festival in the Assembly Room, Belfast, 10–13 July 1792 *Impression by J. Carey*	105
Pony-races at the Theatre Royal, Crowe Street *Engraving*	106
Rustic pastime *Ink drawing*	108
Hurling match *Ink drawing*	109
Bathing and bathing-boxes on the shore at Ringsend *Detail from an oil-painting by Thomas Snagg (1746–1812)*	111

THE ILLUSTRATIONS

Spinning and reeling linen yarn *Engraving of a drawing by William Hincks, 1783*	113
Peasantry—the market *Aquatint by James Malton*	114
Turf footers *Aquatint by James Malton*	116
Cottier's cabin *Engraving from Young, Tour in Ireland*	116
Peasant with spade and shoes in hand *William Harvey, Original Pen and Ink Sketches of the Irish Peasantry, c. 1850*	120
Pig-drover *B. Clayton, Drawing Book of Irish Scenery, Figures, Cattle, etc.*	121
Labourer *B. Clayton, Drawing Book of Irish Scenery, Figures, Cattle, etc.*	122
Peasant with hayfork *Lithograph by A. Murphy, 1824*	123
Barefooted girl in cottage interior, west Galway *Engraving from Hall, Ireland, its Scenery, Character, etc.*	125
Farmer and child *B. Clayton, Drawing Book of Irish Scenery, Figures, Cattle, etc.*	127
Emigrants on the Quays, Cork, *c. 1840 From an oil-painting*	129
Street scene: stage-coach *Detail from an oil-painting by William Turner, 1820*	130–31
Taking up a passenger *A print of a Bianconi coach, 1836*	133
View of Kells, 1819 *Water-colour by George Petrie*	134
Elephant in the Dublin Zoological Gardens *Engraving from the Dublin Penny Journal, 29 August 1835*	135
William Belcher, M.D. and family, with Miss Jane Waring *Silhouette portrait group by Augustin Edouart, 1835*	136
Mulholland's linen mill, Belfast, *c. 1840 Engraving*	136
Sedan-chair and bearers *Detail from a water-colour copy, c. 1920, of an old print*	137
Interior of a Belfast linen-spinning mill *Engraving from Hall, Ireland, its Scenery, Character, etc.*	138
Four hundred people at Mass kneeling round an ark at Kilbaha Beach, 1857 *Engraving*	139
Plan of a workhouse *Drawing from Hall, Ireland, its Scenery, Character, etc.*	141
Dancing at a fair *Drawing, probably early nineteenth-century*	142
Christmas morning in an Irish country shop: giving the customary presents *Drawing by William Brunton*	145
Opening of the Dublin and Kingstown Railway, 1834 *Lithograph*	147
Belfast water-cart *Detail from a water-colour, c. 1870*	148
Inside a public house, 1860 *Oil-painting by J. Noonan*	149
James's Gate Brewery, 1867 *Print*	151
Eviction scene, Vandaleur Estate, co. Clare *Lawrence Collection*	153

THE ILLUSTRATIONS

Farmhouse and family, Clongorey, co. Kildare *Lawrence Collection*	155
Shop and post-office, Nobber, co. Meath *Lawrence Collection*	156
The bicycle in rural Ireland *Photograph taken of three ladies in west co. Limerick, c. 1900–10*	157
Ellison Street, Castlebar *Lawrence Collection*	158
An early motor car in front of the Spa Hotel Restaurant, Lucan *Lawrence Collection*	159
Meadovale Creamery, Charleville, co. Cork *Lawrence Collection*	160
Children outside Carbury National School, co. Kildare *Lawrence Collection*	161
Spriggers at work, Ardara, co. Donegal *Welch Collection*	163
The port of Dublin in the 1880s *From a calendar reproduction*	164–5
A Dublin carter, New Row *Lawrence Collection*	167
Workers leaving shipbuilding yards, Queen's Island, Belfast *Welch Collection*	168
Dublin slum, Poole Street *Lawrence Collection*	171

I

A Rural World

Man first reached Ireland as he advanced into the North of Europe, following the receding fringe of the great glaciers that had once covered much of the Continent. The Palaeolithic or Old Stone Age was over; man brought to Ireland a culture described by archaeologists as Mesolithic or Middle Stone Age. The Mesolithic period was marked by some advances in the techniques of producing tools and weapons of stone. The first Mesolithic men reached Ireland at the beginning of the sixth millennium BC (6000 BC) across the narrow sea between the north-east and Britain. As navigation improved, wider contacts developed until almost four millennia after man's first arrival in Ireland the island was linked up with many countries by a traffic skirting the coasts of Iberia, Brittany, the British Isles and Scandinavia.

During these first four millennia the growth of civilization was slow and painful. The first settlements and their successors were modest in numbers no less than technology. Even at the end of the Mesolithic period (around 3000 BC) there may have been only a few thousand inhabitants in the island. A major impediment to advance was climatic conditions, which resulted in dense forest growth. Settlement was therefore largely confined to sandy soils, river banks, lake shores and, inland, to ground above 500 feet, where forest growth was weaker. It was only in the third millennium BC and with greater sureness in the second millennium that man in now larger numbers began to make inroads into the forests, and even then for the most part in areas such as the Boyne Valley where the river gave access to the interior and where the absence of strong forest growth on the hills of sand and gravel made settlement easier. Primitive technology continued to limit man's ability to convert his environment to his advantage. Tools of stone, even the polished ones of the Neolithic period (3000–2000 BC) were of limited use for felling trees, or for breaking up the soil to plant grain seeds. The advent of the Bronze Age around 2000 BC did not lighten man's tasks. The metal was expensive—the tin to mix with native copper had to be imported and this confined its use to warlike and artistic purposes. In any event, bronze was too soft a metal for effective tools, and stone implements therefore remained common throughout the Bronze Age.

Nevertheless, man, relying on techniques which filtered into native civilization from abroad, had made advances. By Neolithic times he no longer relied exclusively on the fruits of hunting, fishing and trapping, but had begun to supplement his diet by planting grain and by caring for domesticated animals on land won from the forests. Textile fabrics were also being woven, and his dress was therefore no longer hides and skins. In the Bronze Age metal-working skills developed rapidly, Ireland emerging as a main centre of the activity in the north-west of Europe.

With the help of rising population, the isolated communities of former times grew into societies, which, as the archaeological evidence of the so-called megaliths or tombs on sites such as the bend of the Boyne at Newgrange suggests, were marked by a considerable degree of economic and social organization. These burial chambers were covered by a great mass of stone and earth. The great megalith of Newgrange is 300 feet in diameter and almost 50 feet high. In economic terms the building of the megaliths, no less than the transport of the great slabs of stone forming the inner ring of horizontal slabs retaining the mass of earth and stones and the outer ring of isolated standing stones, presupposed a large and highly organized labour force. The emergence of a social system able to support a ruling and priestly caste, and at the same time to maintain the labour employed in impressive feats of building and transport, necessarily depended on the production of a food surplus adequate for the needs of the *élite* and of the megalith-builders. For the first time a food surplus existed.

Grain was, however, still unimportant in the diet, for the advance of cultivation was limited by the inadequacies of stone digging implements. Moreover, despite the fashioning of bronze utensils, the sickle was unknown, suggesting that the harvesting of the crop no less than its sowing was time-consuming. The food surplus must therefore have taken the form of large herds of domesticated cattle, which, as at the bend of the Boyne, were pastured on lands recently won from the forest or on the grassy hills of glacial deposit that outcropped the forests. With the emergence of this wealth, hunting and trapping must have become a recreation rather than a source of livelihood. Life was more sedentary; it left man with more time to fashion ornaments and implements of bronze and to honour his dead by building memorials or by performing ritual ceremonies at these sites.

But with dense forest growth except on higher ground, and with no radical change in the tools for clearing forest and breaking the soil, it was only rising numbers that made possible the extension of the area of settlement. The progress of settlement was necessarily slow. But changing climatic conditions in the first millennium BC, resulting in weakening forest growth and in a fall in the forest line, greatly facilitated the spread of settlement and its intensification in areas already thinly settled. A field system emerged around habitation sites, and the introduction

Stag caught in a trap

of the sickle facilitated the harvesting of grain crops in the new fields. The consumption of grain spread: querns for grinding grain are a common find in the excavation of archaeological sites of this period. The herds of domesticated animals also increased. On excavated sites the majority of bones are ox-bones, suggesting that hunting and trapping had ceased to be important economic functions.

The use of iron, introduced around 500 BC, offered the prospect of more effective tools but it was only from around AD 100 that its use was general enough to have materially assisted the spread of settlement and arable cultivation. But even before this the market for weapons, utensils and ornaments of bronze and gold had widened greatly. The itinerant smith, common in the Early Bronze Age, had disappeared, showing that local markets were now large enough to keep the smiths in full-time employment on the one site. By AD 100 iron-working also became extensive: iron slag is a common find on excavation sites, testifying to its widespread use and falling costs, which facilitated its substitution for the ruder tools. Iron also made possible advances in other crafts, notably in the working of wood and in carpentry: wooden vessels were to a large extent substituted for pottery.

We know from the archaeological evidence something of the way of life of the early inhabitants of Ireland. But we do not know who these people were. All we know with certainty is that in late prehistoric times the predominant race was a Celtic one. But who the earlier inhabitants, Celtic or non-Celtic, were is a matter of surmise. We know only that the island was open to foreign influences and that the evidence suggests affinities with peoples in Iberia, Brittany and Britain. We do not even know for sure whether the cultural development of the island was accompanied by the forceful intervention of invaders or by more peaceful contacts between new peoples and the existing inhabitants. The archaeological evidence suggests a considerable degree of continuity, and traditions from early historic times of great invasions in prehistoric times exaggerate the element of discontinuity.

The political organization of the island in prehistoric times is little less obscure. The megalithic tombs of the third millennium BC, the great earthworks and hill-forts of the early centuries AD suggest that organized communities existed and in time became more numerous. These communities were small, probably at most a few thousand people, although the stronger ones imposed an overlordship on weaker neighbours. It is significant that, as the extension of settlement brought communities into closer contact, bronze weapons, often elaborately ornamented, become a more common archaeological find, suggesting conflict between different groups of aristocratic warriors, which lasted into the Iron Age and the early centuries AD. Moreover, later traditions of conflict between Ulster and inhabitants of the rest of the island appear to be confirmed by archaeological evidence from the late prehistoric centuries. The Black Pig's Dyke, an earthen dyke incorporating natural features in its extension from Bundoran in co. Donegal to Newry in co. Down, appears to have been built in the early centuries AD as a result of a broad cleavage between the peoples on both sides and as a defence against invaders or cattle-raiders from the south. The organized community or *tuath* was a small rural State. Because the small population of each of the many *tuatha* was spread over a large area, land was still relatively plentiful, although in many areas large forests of diminished extent remained and in badly drained lands the decayed forest growth of earlier millennia had produced the great bog-lands which to this day are the outstanding physical characteristic of the Irish midland plain and its fringes.

Clusters of more than a few dwellings were uncommon. The most common habitation site was the *rath* or ring-fort, consisting of a dwelling surrounded by a circular bank and ditch. In some instances a second and even third bank and ditch were added or the bank was reinforced by a wooden stockade or a wattle fence. The dwellings were rectangular or circular with walls of wattle and daub, in some instances sods, and roofs covered by thatch or reeds. In some areas where stone was plentiful the houses and the enclosing walls were of stone: such sites are known as *cahirs* or *cashels*. The size of the ring-fort varied: in some instances the diameter of the enclosed area is as little as

15 yards, in others as much as 150 yards. Some must have belonged to modestly comfortable farmers, others to families whose retainers lived with them within the enclosure, and others were royal residences. The surrounding bank and ditch offered security against wolves for the cattle often enclosed within the rath, no less than for the sleeping inhabitants. At nightfall the gate in the bank was closed, and a chained dog set to watch. These precautions were observed attentively. In the Penitential of St Columbanus (seventh century) a penance is imposed 'if any one has left the enclosure open during the night'. A seventh-century law tract noted that 'a chained dog, whatever mischief he does in the night shall not be paid for'. The walls of the enclosure, moreover, offered shelter against wind and driving rain, and the habitations were often built against the wall rather than in a central position.

A small number of lake-side families lived in *crannógs*, dwellings built on artificial islands close to the shore. Such families worked their land or minded their cattle on the mainland by day, and at night-time sought the refuge of their island homes. Ring-forts or *crannógs* suggest some degree of affluence or status enjoyed by their inhabitants. There must have been other families who lived among their fields in modest, unprotected dwellings, of which no trace has survived.

For all, however, well-to-do or modest, their homes were comparatively cheerless. Smoke from the fire on a central hearth escaped through a hole in the roof or through the door. In the smoke-filled atmosphere eye afflictions must have been common. Moreover, flimsy construction made conflagration a common hazard. Archaeologists have sometimes been able to detect the outline of a burnt house from the dark ashes left in light soil. For the inhabitants of the early monasteries, fire was, for the same reason, an ever-present threat. Once a fire started it spread rapidly through the monastery. Glendalough was destroyed by fire nine times between 775 and 1071, and Clonmacnoise 13 times between 722 and 1205. Within the house, bones and kitchen refuse were not removed, but covered over with successive layers of clay. At night rush candles gave light. Houses were small. Those of well-to-do families may have been as large as 20 feet by 25, and even aristocratic or royal dwellings can hardly have exceeded 40 or 45 feet in length. An early eighth-century law tract stated that the dwelling of a king within an enclosure 140 feet in diameter was 37 feet long, containing 12 beds. In such conditions even well-to-do families slept in dormitory fashion on beds of straw and hides. Privacy was limited and people lived in constant hourly contact with the rest of the family, with retainers and with the activities that revolved around the home. A description of what was to be avoided in a house where a sick man lay, gives an idea of the routine of daily life in the early eighth century:

Burnt outline of hut in Grange Ring-fort

> No games are played in the house. No tidings are announced. No children are chastised. Neither women nor men exchange blows. There is no fighting. The patient is not suddenly awakened. No conversation is held across him or across his pillow. No dogs are set fighting in his presence or in his neighbourhood outside. No shout is raised. No pigs grunt. No brawls are made. No cry of victory is raised nor shout in playing games. No shout or scream is raised.

The family included foster-children, as fosterage was the normal practice in bringing up the young, and children were sent away to be looked after by another family of corresponding position. Foster-children fitted into the social and economic life of the home. According to the early law tracts, boys of the humbler ranks were to be taught the herding of animals, kiln-drying, wool-combing and wood-cutting; girls, grinding with the quern, kneading and sieving. Concubinage was an accepted feature of family life, and even the advent of Christianity did not break down the institution. A concubine, once a child was born to her, acquired the status of a lawful second wife, and the law tracts devoted much attention to relations between the two wives. The recognition of the right of the concubine, where her rights were at stake, to 'inflict damage with her finger-nails and to utter insults and scratchings and hair-tearings and small injuries in general' on the first wife, who had, if wronged, an even greater freedom of replying in kind, gives an impression of a society in which the forceful expression of emotions was taken for granted.

A field system was now well established around habitation sites. But much land, even in settled areas, was still unenclosed. Between May and November, when crops were growing, cattle were led away to summer pastures, and where animals still remained, crops were protected by temporary enclosures which were removed when the harvest was over. With little enclosure, cattle and sheep were generally herded, often with the help of a dog: 'it is a maxim in the law of the Feini that every kind of cattle should have a herdsman by day and by night'. Herding was also necessary to ward off wolves. A seventh-century text stated that 'he who kills a dog that guards the flocks or stays in the house shall pay five cows for the dog and supply a dog of the same breed and restore whatever wild animals eat from the flock until the end of the year'. At night-time cattle and sheep were often driven into the security of the ring-fort: indeed a law tract stated that 'they should be in an enclosure at the fall of night'.

Social status was determined by the ownership or herding of cattle. Trade was limited to ornaments and luxuries in demand among the well-to-do, and a handful of essential items such as salt. Moreover, much of this trade was transacted at the periodic assemblies rather than on a continuous basis. The assemblies of the rulers of *tuatha* or of over-kings, while largely political or ritual, had thus a commercial function, providing the rare occasions on which any large

Man on horseback

Horsemen and chariot

amount of trade or exchange took place. The absence of a coinage—cattle and female slaves were the accepted measure of value—reflects a basically subsistence economy within the *tuath*. Within the circle of family and servants, grain was ground, barley malted and brewed in small vats into ale, animals killed and meat salted for the winter, and even timber burned to provide charcoal for domestic iron-working. Payments for the services of the learned professions or of the skilled crafts were in kind, and were simplified by the fact that for aristocratic families such men were often retainers, rewarded by hospitality, maintenance and gifts.

There were no towns. The only focal points for the community were, apart from the sites of the periodic assemblies, the residences of the rulers. The sites of the residences of the more important rulers are still marked by considerable earthworks. At Tara two ring-forts are surrounded by a fosse and bank outside, almost 900 feet in diameter. Outside this great enclosure is another large earthwork, misnamed the Banqueting Hall, 750 feet by 90 feet. Such extensive works point to a site of considerable importance, the centre, probably, of a small confederation of States in and around co. Meath in the early centuries AD.

Other sites from the same centuries are Eamhain Macha in Ulster, Cruachain in Connaught and Knockaulin in co. Kildare, the site of the royal residence of Ailenn. Roads, except in bog-land, were built and maintained with little expenditure of labour and materials. Rivers were traversed by fords. A fifth-century ecclesiastical document, requiring that 'a monk and a virgin, the one from one place, the other from another, shall not take lodging in the same inn, nor travel in the same carriage from village to village', gives the impression that some facilities for the traveller already existed. The monasteries themselves, which generally maintained a guest-house, must, as they became numerous in the sixth and seventh centuries, have greatly added to these facilities. The use of chariots and ox-drawn carts suggests a carriageway of sorts, although roads were at best but rough tracks making travel slow and disagreeable.

The advent of Christianity, by resulting in a remarkable development of monastic life, brought some diversity into rural Ireland. But in essence the monastery was identical with the larger ring-forts. Monastic buildings and huts of wattle and daub were crowded within an enclosing wall of stone or earth. However, their reputation for learning and piety attracted students, and the larger monasteries, while still small communities, were the nearest approach in early Ireland to towns. It was the relative populousness of the monasteries that gave them leadership in the development of agriculture and in the patronage and the practice of learning and the arts. Their importance as centres of pilgrimage, where they could boast an illustrious founder, added to their revenues and social function, and the lives of the founders were written or rewritten with the customary exag-

Foundation of monastery of Clonmacnoise, sixth century

geration of the saint's miraculous powers in order to promote this side of their activity.

Within each *tuath* society was dominated by family ties and by a well-defined social hierarchy. Although personal ownership of property, including land, existed, property might be alienated to persons outside the family only with the consent of the members of an extended family group of four generations (*derbhfine*). Reflecting the narrow horizons of this rural world, even professions and crafts were hereditary within certain families: the right to abbacies themselves often came to be restricted to members of a particular powerful family. This intense family attitude was accompanied necessarily by a hierarchical one, in which a man's status was determined by the status of the family into which he was born. Indeed, the fine distinctions made in the law tracts, though too minute to be enforceable, testify to the depth of the interest in status and in its definition.

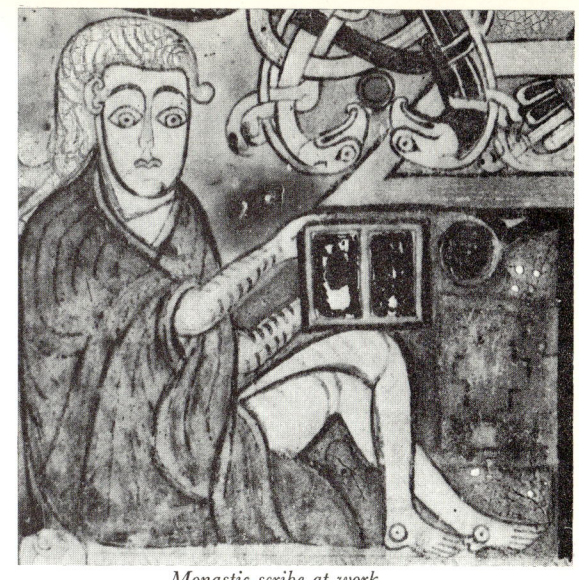

Monastic scribe at work

At the centre of the social system of the *tuath* stood the ruler and the family group eligible for royal office. According to the law, any male within the degree of kinship of four generations to a ruler was eligible for selection by the assembly of freeman of the *tuath*. The freemen consisted of the *flatha* or noblemen, and of non-noble freemen. Nobility itself depended on the possession of dependent freemen (*céili*), and the degree of nobility was determined by their number. In theory, the minimum number of dependants for noble status was ten, and the highest grade of noble had at least 40 dependants. The non-noble freemen owned land, but accepted the status of *céile* by taking cattle from a *flaith*. This was from an economic point

Cleric bearing pastoral staff and bell

of view to the mutual advantage of *flaith* and freemen. The *flaith*'s wealth, measured in cattle, was larger than he could supervise personally, and the *céile* needed cattle to stock his land, which would otherwise not be used to best advantage. The *céile* paid a rent in cattle for the stock given to him, also paid a food rent and supplied labour to the nobleman, and attended him on ceremonial occasions or on military hostings. There were two categories of *céile*, the *soercéile*, who retained his rights as a freeman and participated in the assembly of the *tuath*, and the *doercéile*, who for the duration of their relationship entrusted his rights as freeman into the hands of the noble. *Flatha* and *céilí* between them were the main element in rural society.

The importance of the learned professions and of the skilled crafts is reflected in the fact that they were exercised by freemen. The learned professions, *breitheamh* (lawyer), *file* (literary man), and in pagan times, druid, had an especial privileged position, as in their case alone was their status recognized outside their own *tuath*. The services of leeches or medical men were also well recognized and payment for their services was regarded as part of the compensation due by a guilty party in respect of injuries inflicted. Their skills already attempted to cure a wide range of ills: 'doctors of the body also compound their medicines in diverse kinds', declared the seventh-century Penitential of St Columbanus, 'thus they heal wounds in one manner, sicknesses in another, boils in another, bruises in another, festering sores in another, eye diseases in another, bones in another'. As society advanced, the number of skilled crafts grew. In early Christian times, the industrial crafts were those of house-builders, shipbuilders, millwrights, chariot-makers, turners, leather-workers, fishermen, smiths and metal-workers. By no means all the inhabitants of the *tuath* were of freeman status. Practitioners of the inferior crafts, landless men and tenant occupiers were unfree.

Warrior with spear and shield

Unfree status should not, however, be confused with slavery, an important institution in society and in the economy. In the fourth and fifth centuries, prisoners brought back from Britain by Irish raiding parties were sold into slavery. St Patrick was first brought to Ireland in this way, and spent six years tending flocks. The advent of Christianity did not abolish slavery: the institution survived and was still important as late as the twelfth century. Gang chains found in a royal *crannóg* in co. Meath (AD 900) testify to conditions hard enough to make slaves want to escape, and to severe discipline. St Patrick, speaking of the tribulations of the early Christians in Ireland, stated: 'but the women who are kept in slavery suffer especially; they constantly endure even unto terrors and threats'. Women slaves were especially prized, because they could perform a host of domestic and household tasks in and around well-to-do noble or non-noble households. Like cattle, they became a measure of value, and an acceptable means of payment. A conventional rate of exchange was established between female slaves and cattle: six heifers or three milch cows were the equivalent of a female slave.

We know little of the condition of the mass of the people. Two factors, the extent of warfare, and the adequacy and reliability of the food supply, are, however, likely to have been decisive in determining their general condition. There is much evidence from the Late Bronze Age and from the Iron Age of the multiplication of ornamented weapons, suggesting a war-like aristocracy. Hill-forts and some of the more elaborate earthworks also testify to some element of insecurity, and the souterrains or underground chambers, while in many cases simply chambers for food storage, were in some instances built as a refuge. However, warfare was in part an aristocratic affair. Much of it in any event simply consisted of forays to raid cattle from a neighbouring State. The fact that on many sites the archaeological finds include no weapons suggests that many of the ordinary people led a life in which resort to violence was not contemplated. Warfare may have lessened in early historic times: many of the great earthworks such as Tara were abandoned in the sixth and seventh centuries; standing armies which may have been retained by some of the more warlike rulers in earlier centuries no longer existed; and the laws, first committed to writing in the late seventh or early eighth century, contain no reference to a military profession.

Thus warfare can hardly have affected the ordinary man very greatly, and for the cattle-owning aristo-

Seventh-century warrior with sword and shield

cracy it probably provided an outlet for their high spirits and rapacity. The food supply was in all probability a much more important factor. It is likely indeed that the diet of the mass of the people was in some respects more adequate than in later times. Meat was probably eaten by all classes in late prehistoric and early historic times. However, the supply had its limitations. Animals were invariably left out of doors even in winter, no hay was saved from the summer growth of grass and the animals must have been very undernourished in winter. Meat, in salted form, was known as 'winter food' as opposed to the 'summer food', which was largely dairy produce. In winter-time the supply of milk from the badly undernourished milch cows would have been extremely meagre. Repeated winters of undernourishment meant that animals were not only undersized by comparison with modern animals, but that their general condition was indifferent. As such, their resistance to disease was poor, and cattle diseases, which were well known to the community, must at times have played havoc with the herds. The result was that, large though the herds were, food deficiencies still existed. As the population grew or as numbers of people congregated together in more populous centres such as the monasteries, efforts were therefore made to vary the food supply.

Monk with book

The development of arable cultivation owed much to the monasteries. By the seventh century grain, rather than butter, milk and meat, appears to have been the main item in monastic diet, and outside the monasteries grain was acquiring a more important place in the dietary. A more plentiful supply of grain also made possible the production of much greater quantities of ale from barley. Ale brewed in the home or in the monastery was commonplace, and drunkenness was already a condition with which both the penitentials and the law tracts dealt. Every monastery was a centre of agricultural activity. It had its own lay dependants or *céili*, and supplemented its own labour supply, that of the monks, by labour services rendered by its *céili*. Significantly, in the language of the day, even labour services rendered by a lay dependant to a lay lord came to be known as *manchuine* or monastery labour.

With the growing importance of grain in the economy and in the diet, the rotary quern ceased to be adequate for grinding and water-driven mills made their appearance. The craft of millwright emerged as a specialized skill in its own right. The first water-driven mills were introduced in the seventh century, probably by the monasteries. Nobles soon came to be mill-owners as well, and while the building of a mill was generally beyond the resources of the non-noble freemen, they sometimes came together to build and run one in partnership. The mills were very active after the harvest: the laws dealt with matters such as precedence and in the ninth century the Church expressly prohibited grinding on Sundays. Grain yields were, however, low: the poor quality of the livestock and the inadequate feeding combined to result in a deficient supply of manure for the land.

In a favourable year the Irishman of early historic times was almost certainly better fed than his counterpart of medieval or early modern times. But in a closed community such as the rural Ireland of these centuries, trade in grain was limited and in a year of failure there was little likelihood of a local shortage being made good by grain brought from elsewhere. In any event, harvest failure tended to be general rather than localized. Only in later times, with the development of foreign trade, did the possibility arise of relieving the distress caused by bad harvests through imports of grain from abroad. Foreign trade was very limited. Although wine was better known in early Christian times, the importance of ale as the beverage even of the upper classes was, if anything, enhanced.

The organization of the economy was simple. Internal trade was limited, much of it being transacted as an adjunct to the assemblies held periodically at a large number of sites. There was no merchant class as such, and the law tracts of the early eighth century confirm this picture of narrow trade and no trading class. The only substantial industrial buildings of early historic Ireland were the

Harp player

mills: significantly, the law tracts in the case of the mills alone define their construction, specifying eight parts of a mill. Society reflected economic organization. The rulers were themselves large cattle-owners. Even a ruler's immediate followers were occupied seasonally in agriculture: a law tract of the eighth century noted the seed-sowing season as the one season in which a king went forth with a company of only three.

The ruler of a *tuath* personally looked after affairs rather than depended on an administration. Writing was not introduced until the advent of the Christian era in the fifth century, and the laws themselves were not committed to writing till the seventh or eighth century. The simple nature of a king's administration and the rural background against which he exercised his authority are suggested in the seven occupations indicated in an eighth-century law tract as befitting a king: 'Sunday for drinking ale, for he is not a lawful chief who does not distribute ale every Sunday; Monday for judgment, for the adjustment of the people; Tuesday at chess; Wednesday, seeing greyhounds coursing; Thursday at marriage duties [i.e. ceremonies]; Friday at horse-racing; Saturday at giving judgments.'

The culture, knowledge and learning of this society were interwoven with the great folk-tales of early historic Ireland (some of which survive in later written versions), handed down from one generation to the next and within each generation repeated orally many times over. It was not surprising that story-telling was not only the way of transmitting learning and law, but in the folk-tales of heroic deeds by aristocratic rural warriors a source of entertainment in which the *naïveté* and rich imagination of a rural community were satisfied in images familiar to them from their everyday life. The telling of tales, a brand of game akin to chess, hunting, trapping and in less settled areas or times cattle-raiding were the main entertainments of the upper classes. Music was also important, and harpers alone among musicians enjoyed the status of freemen. The assemblies, while occasions for the transaction of the public business of the *tuath* and for athletic sports and horse-riding, were also occasions of music.

Simple though the economy was, it was capable of advance —the development of arable cultivation, in part due to the pressure of population, in part to the monasteries, is witness to this. But what advance took place did nothing to alter the rural nature of the country. Trade, except at the periodic fairs, continued to stagnate. Despite some measure of population growth, there was no tendency for town life to develop. Striking evidence of the extent to which this was a self-sufficient economy was the absence of urban development on the coast. It was thus a closed society, and it is significant that the only wide contact of the island with the outside world, the exodus of monks and scholars which helped to revitalize Britain and Europe after the Barbarian invasions, sprang solely from the ascetism of the monks and from exile, self-imposed as a penance or sacrifice, from familiar and loved surroundings.

Further Reading

L. Bieler, *Ireland, harbinger of the Middle Ages*, 1963
M. Dillon (ed.), *Early Irish society*, 1954
M. Duignan, 'Irish agriculture in early Christian times' in *Journal of the Royal Society of Antiquaries of Ireland*, vol. LXXIV, pt. 3, 1944
M. Duignan and Lord Killanin, *Shell Guide to Ireland*, 1967
F. Henry, *Early Christian Irish art*, 1963
—— *L'art irlandais* (3 vols), 1963–64
—— *Irish art in the early Christian period*, 1965
K. Hughes, *The Church in early Irish society*, 1966
T. W. Moody and F. X. Martin (ed.), *The course of Irish history*, 1967
S. P. O'Riordain, *Antiquities of the Irish countryside*, 1966
M. and L. de Paor, *Early Christian Ireland*, 1958
J. Raftery, *Prehistoric Ireland*, 1951
—— (ed.), *The Celts*, 1964
F. J. Byrne, *Irish kings and high kings*, 1972

II

Conflict in Ireland: the Old Order and the New Towns 800–1550

The relative peace and stability of Irish society was shattered at the outset of the ninth century by the sudden appearance on the Irish coasts of the Norsemen, seafaring invaders from Scandinavia. The principal monasteries—in the absence of towns the only centres of wealth—were destroyed time and time again. The security of Irish monastic life broken, there was a further exodus of monks, this time motivated by the quest of more secure living conditions.

The Norsemen had necessarily to establish bases on the Irish coasts for their incursions into the interior: their long clinker-built ships were drawn up on the shore above the water-line and behind the security of an earthern bank and ditch beyond. In time some of these encampments developed into small settled communities and, where other circumstances were favourable, into the first towns. Dublin was the largest of the Norse settlements. Within its walls, each town was a tight huddle of houses. There were no large open spaces: in Dublin the assembly mound or thing-motte stood outside the walls. Though most of the houses were built of clay and wattles, there were also some houses built of stone. In Dublin, in the later years of the settlement at any rate, both its ruler, the Jarl, and its overking, the King of Leinster, had residences of stone within the walls.

The Norsemen stand out in Irish history not only as the

founders of the first towns but as builders of stone edifices and as merchants. Building in stone advanced rapidly in the ninth and tenth centuries. The Irish imitated the new techniques: much of the vocabulary of house-building in Irish is of Scandinavian origin. Monastic buildings of stone became more common. In particular the distinctive round towers, built possibly as observation points or as centres of refuge, were raised on many of the monastic sites. Moreover, the maritime contacts of the Norse with their homeland and with communities of Scandinavian origin along the western coasts of Europe resulted in a considerable expansion of overseas trade. As conditions became less warlike and as Norse contacts with the Irish outside the settlements multiplied, the development of trade was all the more marked: the first coinage in Ireland appeared in Dublin early in the eleventh century.

The armed conflict brought on by the Norsemen's raids led to greater cruelty and violence in the country at large. In imitation of Norse practice, the mutilation or blinding of hostages and rivals became a common form of revenge among the Irish. The settled Norse communities, in growing contact with the Irish as a result of political alliance with native rulers or their domestic rivals, and even intermarriage, in time turned to Christianity. By the early eleventh century the Norse towns were subordinate kingdoms acknowledging allegiance to Irish overlords. But the Norse settlements were still distinctive: their merchant oligarchies contrasted with the rural aristocracy

Composition of a book at Kildare

Two knights in armour

of Irish kingdoms; and through the consecration of their bishops in England, their Church was part of the English rather than of the Irish Church.

The Norse towns powerfully promoted the growth of trade. The brisk trade in slaves from Bristol conducted by them helped to perpetuate the institution of slavery. They also introduced new products such as silks, and with their greatly superior shipping expanded what had been a very small trade in wine. The Welshman, Giraldus, visiting Ireland in the 1180s in the wake of the conquering Normans, was impressed by the market for wine: 'imported wines however, conveyed in the ordinary commercial way, are so abundant that you would scarcely notice that the vine was neither cultivated nor gave its fruit there'. Within the country the commercial activity at the fairs was better defined than in the past. Some impression of it is given in a poem from the eleventh century describing the fair of Carman:

> *Three busy markets on the ground,*
> *A market of food, a market of livestock,*
> *The great market of the Greek strangers,*
> *Wherein is gold and fine raiment.*

Expansion beyond the confines of the *tuath* was a more common ambition of Irish rulers: it led also to a new concept of kingship with aspirations to the extension of overlordship to the whole island. Brian Boru, King of the Dail gCais in co. Clare, in having himself described in Armagh in 1005 in the great Book of Armagh as *imperator Scottorum* or Emperor of the Irish, testifies to this novel concept, which influenced the ambitions and activities of the more powerful Irish kings of the eleventh and twelfth centuries. The initial shock of the Norse invasions had furthered this development, because the necessity of resistance to the challenge represented by the Norse made Irish rulers more conscious of the need to increase their military strength and expand their overlordship. There was no intention of ousting the Norse from the island. While on occasion the

Norse were the enemies of Irish rulers, they were also on many occasions, even before their settlements had been reduced to subordinacy, useful allies. Indeed, because of their wealth in ships the Norse towns themselves proved invaluable allies against other Norse settlements. The alliance of Dublin with its greater wealth and more strategic position was especially important, and an awareness of this was evident in the policy of Irish rulers in the eleventh and twelfth centuries.

The new political ambitions of Irish rulers were, however, frustrated by the Norman invasion from 1169, resulting in the extension of lordship by the King of England to the island. Nominal for much of the country, it was effective at first in the east, north, south-east and south of the island. On their conquered lands, the first castles or forts of the Normans were simple structures of the motte and bailey type—an enclosure for cattle and retainers and a raised mound topped by a platform of wood were both surrounded by a dyke filled with water. They were soon followed by stone structures.

The Normans took over the existing towns, and Dublin, which became the main administrative centre of the Norman kingdom, was already pre-eminent among Irish towns. New towns were also founded in the eastern half of the country, and in the extreme west at Galway and Athenry. In particular, many new towns were founded in the river valleys of the south-east, including Rosponte or *villa novi pontis* at New Ross, where a bridge was thrown across the wide span of the Barrow.

The importance of the towns was enhanced by the failure of the Normans to hold all the land they had conquered in the twelfth and thirteenth centuries. In Ulster and Connaught nothing at all remained of the colony by the fifteenth century apart from a few towns. Even in Leinster the colony was severely harassed by Irish chief-

Suitors before the Court of Exchequer

Irish kings

tains, who began to push out from the forests, marshes and mountains in which even at the peak of the colony in the thirteenth century they had never been crushed. In 1372 the Council of the Anglo-Norman lordship was reduced to offering Donnchadh MacMurchadha 20 marks as his price for 'the safe keeping of the royal roads between Carlow and Kilkenny'. However, this did not purchase security for the colony. In 1391 an armourer was engaged to dwell in Carlow at a wage of a shilling a day for three months 'to make arms against the Irish then proposing to destroy the town'. By the late fifteenth century the extent of the Norman lordship in Leinster, apart from some towns, was reduced to part of the four counties surrounding the city of Dublin. This was a small area about 30 miles by 20, which came to be known as the Pale and which, according to a Statute passed by a Parliament in 1495, was to be surrounded by the inhabitants with a double ditch, six feet high on the part 'which mereth next unto Irishmen'.

CONFLICT IN IRELAND: OLD ORDER AND NEW TOWNS

Given the incompleteness of the Norman conquest, a long-drawn-out contest between Irish and Norman was inevitable. Such conflict was not, however, a straightforward one between the two races. Within the Anglo-Norman lordship the administration was only partially effective. Lawlessness frequently degenerated into open conflict between rival Norman magnates and their retainers, and especially in the 'marches' (i.e. the areas in which the writ of English law was incompletely established) conflict with the Irish was simply a confused extension of internal conflict in which the Irish entered as allies or foes of the contending parties. The Irish, after the initial stages, were able to resist the new settlers with much more success. Creton, a French nobleman who accompanied the second expedition of King Richard II to Ireland in 1399, noted: 'wilder people I never saw; they did not appear to be much dismayed at the English'. The characteristic Irish weapon was the axe, adopted from the Norse. Giraldus Cambrensis in the twelfth century had related how 'from an old and evil custom they always carry an axe in their hand as if it were a staff. In this way, if they have a feeling for any evil, they can the more quickly give it effect . . . without further preparation, beyond being raised a little, it inflicts a mortal wound.'

The Irish chieftains in the thirteenth and fourteenth centuries imported axe-carrying *galloglaigh* or gallowglasses—mercenaries of mixed Irish-Scandinavian ancestry from the Scottish islands.

Whole colonies of these mercenaries were settled in the north, and along with Irish mercenaries equipped in imitation of them, greatly added to the fighting effectiveness of the native chieftains. The conflict between the two races was by no means a purely military one. The benefits of English Common Law were not extended to the mass of Irish living within the Anglo-

Use of the axe

Irish gallowglasses or mercenaries

Norman lordship, and an effort was made to remove Irishmen from offices in Church, State or town. This resulted in a measure of retaliation. An attempt in the fourteenth century to substitute English bishops for Irish and to prevent the promotion of Irishmen to Cathedral chapters resulted in the Irish monasteries banning English postulants.

Ireland was now divided into two distinct social orders—a Norman or English order in the towns and in a receding extent of countryside beyond the towns, and an Irish one in areas outside, some of which had never been conquered by the Normans and others of which had been won back in the military recovery of the Irish. Within the English lordship the English Common Law was applied; outside, the Irish or 'brehon' laws, 'which rightly ought not to be called law, being bad custom', and in the marches or frontier areas, march law, an amalgam of Irish and English law. Outside, Irish was the universal tongue. Inside, Norman-French in earlier times or later, English, was the spoken language: the language of the Statutes until 1495 was in fact French or Latin only. The walled towns of the English were also a contrast with the villages of the Irish area 'surrounded with wood, palisades and stagnant

Hill-top residence of the O'Hagans at Tullaghoge

water', as the French chronicler Froissart's informant, Henry Castide, described an Irish township. To the Normans and English, the active trade of their towns and the fact that the market for food that they created made the Norman agriculture of the surrounding rural areas a market-orientated one, seemed to imply a lack of interest in trade on the part of the Irish. Giraldus Cambrensis, whose account in the twelfth century reflected the opinion of the first Norman settlers, thought that 'this people despises agriculture, has little use for the money making of towns, contemns the rights and privileges of citizenship'. Centuries later Andrew Borde, an English writer of Early Tudor times, informed his readers that 'the people ther be slothful, not regarding to sow and tille theyr landes, nor caring for riches'.

But though conflict and contrast divided the two societies, the differences were never total and narrowed in the course of time. Many of the members of the Anglo-Norman

Sir John Moriz, Deputy Governor in Ireland for Edward III, 1346

Inauguration ceremony of an Irish chieftain (O'Neill), c. 1600

lordship, choosing to ignore the sharp distinction that the often ineffective administration in Dublin sought to draw between the two races, adopted the Irish language and customs. As the Irish military revival brought warfare to areas which had for a time been peaceful, many of the Anglo-Norman inhabitants left the disturbed countryside for the security of the towns or left the island altogether. The reduced numbers remaining were all the more prone to adopt Irish ways. The laws against adopting the Irish language and way of life were not the result of racial hatred so much as of an anxiety to avoid the erosion of the power of the lordship in large areas by the Hibernicization of their Anglo-Norman inhabitants. These were the 'degenerate English' of the marches, who, in contrast to the loyal English of the towns and obedient shires, adopted Irish ways. Even in these latter areas the process was experienced to some extent. It was stated with some exaggeration in 1515 that 'all the king's subjects of the four shires be near hand Irish and wear their habits and use their tongue'. Although within the towns the spoken language was Norman-French and later English, a relatively liberal policy in admitting Irishmen meant that Irish was also heard within the walls and that some of the inhabitants either spoke the language or were acquainted with it.

It is essential, however, not to overlook the fact that the Normans were not alone in changing. The fact is that in growing more alike both the Normans or English and the Irish were changing, and the Irish no less than the Hibernicized Normans, bore only a limited resemblance to their ancestors of two or three centuries previously. The powers of the native chieftains within their States were much greater than in the past, a development reflected in the sixteenth century in a tendency towards primogeniture in the succession to the chieftainship. The dress and appearance of the chieftains also changed greatly, and no longer appeared to the English, as did that of the Irish rulers even as late as the fourteenth century, unpretentious. The English squire, Henry Castide, preparing four Irish kings for knighting by Richard II in Dublin in 1399 had 'great difficulty at first to induce them to wear robes of silken cloth, trimmed with squirrel skin or miniver, for the kings only wrapped themselves up in an Irish cloak'. However, by the sixteenth century the Irish chieftains could be a match in splendour for the English. The Lord Deputy, St Leger, meeting Manus O'Donnell at Cavan in 1540, was greeted by an elegant gentleman magnificently dressed in crimson velvet, whose chaplain was 'a right sober young man well learned and brought up in France'.

The economy in the Irish areas had also become more market-orientated. Remarks such as that of the French nobleman, Creton, inspired by the information that Art MacMorrogh had paid 400 cows for his steed, that 'there is little money in the country, wherefore their usual traffic is only with cows',

Meeting of Art MacMorrogh, King of Leinster, and the Earl of Gloucester

Cattle raid

overlook the fact that trade had already reached deep, though unevenly, into the hinterland of the towns. Such views, moreover, do not represent the opinion of town-dwellers themselves or of policy-makers within the lordship. In 1431 merchants and other subjects were forbidden to frequent Irish fairs and markets 'whereat the enemy take great return and benefits to the depression of our boroughs and trading towns'. Such was the amount of the trade with the Irish that a Parliament in 1463-64 declared that 'as the profit of every city and town in the land depends principally on the resort of Irish people bringing merchandise thereinto, the people of Cork, Waterford, Limerick and Youghal may trade with the Irish, in spite of all statutes contrary'. Moreover, much of the area controlled by the Normans themselves had a rural character. A striking feature of the Anglo-Norman settlement had been the number of rural centres which had the elements of a town constitution granted to them by the lord of the manor but never developed into towns.

The most noteworthy structures in this rural scene were the castles of stone built by the Norman lords and from the fourteenth century onwards by the Irish chieftains in imitation of Norman practice. Norman and Irish lords alike had large numbers of retainers which they quartered oppressively on the inhabitants of the countryside. The castle with its adjoining *bawn* or walled enclosure no less than the retainers was the source of military strength of lord and chieftain. Within it the retainers sheltered in time of danger and the lord's cattle driven within its walls were secure from the cattle raids conducted by rival magnates. The ordinary inhabitants of the countryside were much less secure in the sporadic military rivalry of the magnates of the period, and enjoyed little protection against raid or reprisal. A Tudor source relates how 'when it is daylight they [the chieftains] will go to the poor villages . . . burning the houses and corn and ransacking of the poor cottages. They will drive all the kine and plough horses, with all other cattle and drive them away. . . .'

Despite the presence everywhere of herds of cattle and sheep, arable cultivation was important. Yields were, however, small. 'The crops give great promise in the blade', wrote Giraldus Cambrensis, 'even more in the straw but less in the ear. For here the grains of wheat are shrivelled and small, and can scarcely be separated from the chaff by any winnowing fan'. But for the Normans, yields were also low. On a manor belonging to Christ Church Cathedral, at Clonkeen, co. Dublin, one-quarter of the wheat in the 1344 harvest was allowed for seed. Among the Normans, as among the Irish, grain was often stored along with other goods and valuables within the churches. In 1307, for instance, Sibilla la Gras was involved in a dispute regarding the breaking of a lock on a chest in the Church of Ardart, co. Kerry, 'in which chest Sibilla had one crannoc of wheat, value $\frac{1}{2}$ mark, and three bushels of barley, value 2s'. But there were other more insidious enemies. Giraldus Cambrensis had noted in the twelfth century that 'mice are infinite in number and consume much more grain than anywhere else, as well as eating up garments even though they be locked up carefully'.

Where the Normans colonized, they introduced the open field system known to them in England and Normandy. The arable land of each lord's manor was divided into several great fields, in each of which a three-course rotation of winter crops (wheat or rye), spring corn (oats) and fallow was followed. This system was orientated towards meeting the needs not only of

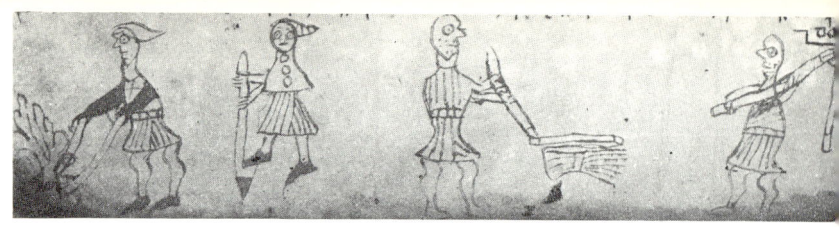

Ploughing, digging and threshing in the fifteenth century

the manor's inhabitants but of the townspeople, and in good years there was often a surplus which was exported. Animal stocks were grazed on the commons and waste, which were often extensive, and on the fallow field or after the harvest on the stubble in the other fields. Sheep-rearing was of especial importance, and under the Normans wool came to be one of the country's main exports.

The manor's freeholders and tenants held their land not in a compact mass, but in strips scattered through the open fields. Immediately below the lord in status were the free tenants, who paid a low or nominal rent for their land, gave military service to the lord, and participated in the manorial court at which the lord presided. Free but less privileged than the free tenants were the *firmarii* or leasehold tenants, who held their land for a duration and rent stipulated by contract. The *firmarii*, some of whom were Irish, farmed comparatively small acreages, but by the standards of the time they enjoyed a modest but definite degree of comfort and ease. Many of them employed house- and farm-servants. In the case of 33 farmers in the co. Dublin area in the second half of the fifteenth century, whose wills survive, the average area under tillage was 18 acres. They had, of course, access to grazing on other land, and oxen, sheep, lambs, hogs, pigs, cart- and farm-horses are enumerated as their stock. In addition they possessed carts, wagons, wheels, ploughs, coulters and yokes. But it is clear at the same time that the margin they enjoyed above subsistence level did not admit of any show of affluence. Their household effects were modest including few, if any, brass pots and other expensive utensils, and rarely expensive garments or plate. Akin to the *firmarii* in some respects were the *gavillers* who held their land not by contract, but by customary tenure.

Below these classes were the *betaghs*, a category not found on all manors. The *betaghs* were almost all of Irish origin, lived in family groups and often worked the land in common. Their peculiar position was often denoted by the fact that the lands they farmed were separate from the open fields of the manor. However, though the *betagh* was tied to the land in the district in which he lived and was, therefore, in a sense a possession of the lord of the manor, the fact that some of the *betaghs* paid much higher rents than some of the *firmarii* suggests that some of them were people of resource and some substance able to take on the task of cultivating larger acreages than many *firmarii*.

Firmarii and *betaghs*, in addition to their money rents, had to perform labour services for the lord. But in contrast to conditions in England, the labour services were comparatively few, and, even for the *betaghs*, had, from the late thirteenth and early fourteenth centuries, been falling in amount and were often replaced by money payments. An instance of the more onerous labour obligations was in Balybothy, co. Tipperary, where in 1415–16 the tenants had to plough for the lord an acre of wheat, an acre of oats, and to give five days reaping, five days weeding and five days carting grain. The scarcity of labour in the countryside, brought about in part by migration from the

Fifteenth-century hunting scene

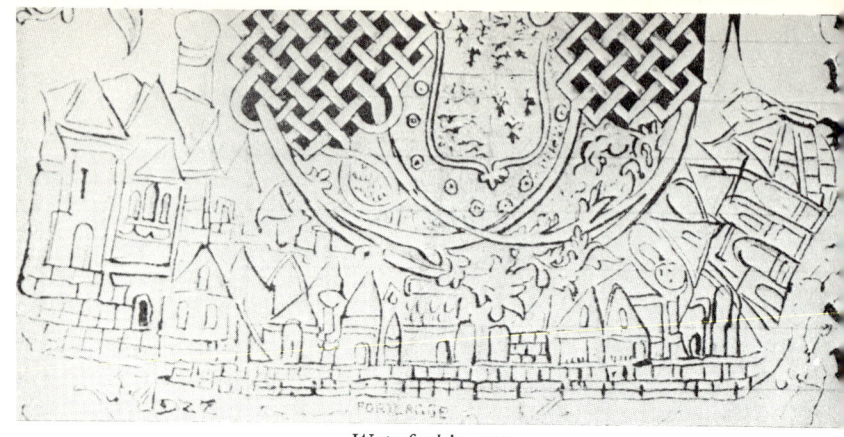
Waterford in 1566

unsettled areas and accentuated by the heavy mortality associated with the Black Death, enabled those remaining to bargain for less onerous conditions. As for the *betaghs*, much of whose wealth lay in cattle, the fact that they could flee along with their chattels to Irish areas, made it necessary for the lord to offer them conditions attractive enough to induce them to stay. A result of the small and declining amount of labour services performed by tenants was that manors came to rely mainly on labour hired by the day for the cultivation of the soil. On the manor belonging to Christ Church Cathedral at Clonkeen, Kill o' the Grange, of the 562 workdays performed by reapers during the 1344 harvest, 471 were done by day-labourers, and only 91 by the customary tenants. The labour force in the countryside could be divided into two categories —labourers whose services were hired by the day and who were often cottiers cultivating a small plot, and permanent servants. The permanent staff of the manor of Clonkeen included a bailiff, serjeant, carter, two ploughmen, two plough-drivers, a door-keeper, a woman 'drying malt and doing other necessary work within the manor', and a cowherd.

In Irish districts land tenure was the same in principle as it had been in early historic times, but it is almost certain that the relative share of the community's land and cattle possessed by the chieftains and their immediate families had grown considerably. Irish agriculture, with its absence of the open-field arrangement, contrasted with the Anglo-Norman areas with the arable lands divided into great fields, each in turn minutely sub-divided and cultivated in accordance with a common crop-rotation. But the feudal land organization generally broke down where the Irish military revival was successful. Moreover, even in areas which were not overrun by the Irish recovery, the exodus of much of the population had contributed to the withdrawing of much land from the open fields through the enclosing of small areas with fences or walls. Even within the Pale there was much enclosure in the fifteenth century. For instance, in Malahide in 1495 Thomas Balle was leased 'four acres more or less of tilling land to make a park'.

The towns were scattered through this rural world, on or close to the coast or along the river valleys, making the sharpest contrast between Norman and Irish ways. 'There be good townes, and cities, as Dublin and Waterford,' wrote the Tudor traveller Andrew Borde, 'where the Englyshe fashion is, as in meate, drinke, other fare and lodging.' Within the walled towns defence was an obligation falling on all the citizens. All the men, including apprentices, were required to possess arms so that they could, when necessary, take their part in the town's defence. The guilds also contributed money on occasion towards the defence of the town. In Dublin in 1575 the Tailors' Guild paid 6s 'for keeping or guarding the gate of the cittie'.

Outside the walls there were suburbs, and the burgesses within the towns often owned land and engaged in farming. Within the town each householder was under an obligation to keep clean the portion of the street before his own door. Sanitary facilities were inadequate, and the problem of cleanliness was as a result all the more difficult. The Council in Galway decreed in 1508 'that whatsoever man, woman or childe, be found foullinge the streets or walls, either by night or

Monks singing psalms

Sixteenth-century ship

day, to lose 2*d*'. The only sanitation consisted of latrines or privies with open drains, and not all houses were so provided. The presence of large numbers of animals within the towns added to the accumulation of filth and created disagreeable smells which often caused concern to the municipal authorities. In Dublin in 1366 slaughtering within the city was prohibited 'to prevent the excessive and noxious stenches hitherto caused by slaughter of cattle in the city'. In Galway in 1509 the municipality decreed that 'whatsoever man or woman have any kyne in towne shall keep them in their houses both summer and winter, and if they be found on the street to pay 4*d* and no swine or goat to be kept in towne above fourteen days, on payn of killing'.

Plague and disease were common in the crowded and often noisome surroundings. The Black Death in the middle of the four-

Net-fishing from a boat

teenth century, which killed unprecedented numbers in country as well as in town, was exceptional. The fact that, under normal circumstances, plague and disease prevailed in town rather than country gave substance to contemporary belief that, as in 1489, 'dung-heaps, swine, hog-sties and other nuisances in the streets, lanes and suburbs of Dublin, infect the air and produce mortality, fevers, pestilence throughout the city'. As a result, when fever was abroad, those who were free to do so avoided the towns. 'The fear of pestilence prevents the coming thither of lords, ecclesiastics and lawyers', it was noted of Dublin in 1489. One of the problems of the towns was ensuring a supply of clean water. In Dublin an aqueduct carried water from an outside source into a central cistern in the city, from whence it was distributed to other outlets within the walls. When the Friars Preachers at the Church of the Holy Saviour were given permission in the thirteenth century to attach a pipe from their property to the citizens' pipe, we read that 'the diameter of the Friars' pipe is to be five inches; within their house, it is to be so far narrowed that its opening may be stopped by the insertion of a man's little finger.'

Fire was another hazard of the towns, and fear that it might occur haunted the inhabitants. Most of the houses were made of wood, and even stone houses commonly had roofs of thatch. As a result fire spread rapidly from house to house. In Dublin in 1457 each house was required to have a container of water beside the door and the Ordinances of the Common Council of the city included one decreeing that 'any person answerable for the burning of a street shall be arrested, cast into the middle of the fire, or pay one hundred shillings'. An Ordinance in Waterford in 1388 went so far as to order the destruction of houses with roofs of thatch or at least of the roofs. This was an extreme measure. In Galway in 1521, for fear of houses near the walls being set alight from outside, it was ordered 'that no man shall build, make or repayre any strawe or tache house for fere of fyre, no nigher the towne walls than fourteen feet unless they be covered with sklatts'. The fact that this order expressly noted that 'both the great stone housses, as Martin and John Lynch is housses and also as John Cayne ys housse to be excepted, iff they cover the same with sklatts' suggests not only that thatch roofs were universal in Galway but that houses of stone were still quite exceptional.

All the towns, especially the sea and river ports, were active centres of trade. Grain, cattle and wool poured into them to meet domestic needs and to sustain an active export business in wool, hides and often in grain. Fishing was also important, and fish supplemented the diet of the citizens and helped to make up export cargoes. Through the ports essential imports such as wine, iron and salt were distributed. But at heart the towns were exclusive in their outlook, and regarded merchants from other towns in Ireland no less than merchants from overseas as foreigners. Outsiders, Irish or foreign, unless they acquired the prized privilege of freemen, were prohibited from dealing in retail trade, from having dealings while they remained within the walls with any save freemen of the town, or indeed from dallying at all in the town for a period exceeding 40 days.

Mayor of Dublin

The towns, as centres of trade and population, were also characterized by a variety of industrial occupations. In Dublin, for instance, there were separate guilds for smiths, barber surgeons, bakers, cooks, tanners, tallow chandlers, glovers and skinners, weavers, carpenters and so on. One of the objects of each town was jealously to guard the market for the members of its own guilds. A by-law of the Common Council of Dublin in 1555, for instance, declared: 'no merchant or outher shall bringe into this cittie to be solde any thinge readie made belonging to any facultie within the cittie, and which the men of that facultie do make and wurke, saving that in the market daie and during the tyme of market it shalbe lawfull for smythes and sho-makers of the countrey to bringe in things of their facultie, as they have used, yeving theirin a cheaper price than the citizen doeth.'

This by-law also illustrates the fact that prices for some commodities were cheaper outside the town than within, and that on that account, despite the general policy of conserving the market for local tradesmen, it was necessary for the municipality, as in this instance, to tolerate trade in goods made up outside. Cheaper labour in the countryside as much as the monopoly tendencies of the guilds were responsible for this disparity in price. A result of this situation was that some sought to take advantage of favourable labour costs outside by putting materials out for execution by workers in the countryside and flouting local regulations by selling the finished articles in the town. The Weavers' Guild in Dublin, for instance, complained in 1580 that 'dyvers free cittezens of this cittie putteth ther worck to forrens to be wrought and don by them'.

Irish townswomen, c. 1575

The function of the guilds was not only economic but social and religious. The members participated in religious ceremonies as a body on their patron saint's feast-day and on certain other days, fines being imposed for absence on certain of these occasions. Alms were also given to needy members. The guilds also provided a certain amount of entertainment for their members. The Tailors' Guild, for instance, in Dublin organized a banquet on the feast of their patron, St John the Baptist, at midsummer: for 1553 their accounts include items such as 'a pc.

of whete agaynste mydsomer to make cakes', 'whyte wyne and clare wyne att mydsomer', 'ale att mydsomer drynking', and 'seke [i.e. sack] the same tyme'. The quarterly general meetings of the Tailors were accompanied by a breakfast, sometimes enlivened by music, one year's accounts containing for this occasion the item 'payd to the mynstralis the daye of Richard taverneres brekeffaste ... XIId'.

One of the most impressive features of Dublin were the great pageants of Mystery plays presented by the guilds. Twenty-eight occupations are mentioned in the municipal regulations of 1498 for the Corpus Christi Pageant, representing various scenes from the Old and New Testaments. The mariners, vintners, ships carpenters and salmon-catchers represented 'Noe, with his shipp apparalid acordying'; the fishermen, the Twelve Apostles; the merchants, the Prophets; and the butchers 'tormentours with their garmentis well and clenly peynted'. The accounts of the Tailors' Guild, who played 'Pilate, with his fellaship, and his lady and his knyghtes well beseyne' include payments in 1554 'to Steven Casse for playnge pilote a Corpis Christi day'. Another pageant took place on St George's Day. The dragon entered into both pageants: it was the duty of 'the hagardmen and the husbandmen to berr the dragoun and to repair the dragoun a Seint Georges day and Corpus Christi day'.

A noblewoman

Giraldus Cambrensis in the twelfth century had stated that illness, with the exception of the ague, was almost unknown in Ireland and that consequently 'the island has little use for doctors'. But one is likely to place little credence in this opinion, and a good deal more in the same author's statement that 'where dangers to health are so very few, so too are the remedies'. Nevertheless, Irish medicine at this time, based apparently on common sense and on the use of herbs, must have had its positive aspects and have proved of some value in the alleviation of pain and illness. The quality of Irish medicine deteriorated during the medieval period. Almost paradoxically, this was due to contact with contemporary medical study on the Continent. As early as 1333 there is record of an Irishman engaged in the study of medicine at the medical school of Montpellier in the south of France. Medical study on the Continent had, by this time, acquired a philosophical and speculative bias. The substitution in many instances of what was no better than superstition for observation and experiment resulted in bizarre teachings, which through medical texts written in Irish, modelled on continental thought, spread through Ireland. For instance, one medical text in the Irish language contained a cure for baldness, which required a jar to be filled with mice, and buried near a fire for a year and advised that when applying it with the hand 'it is urgent that he that shall apply it use a glove lest at his finger-tips the hair begin to sprout'.

In the schools in which medicine was taught, learning was acquired simply by a process of learning by rote. Campion, an English visitor to Ireland in 1571, described the schools of law and medicine in Ireland: 'I have sene them where they kept schoole, ten in some one chamber, groveling upon couches of straw, their bookes at their noses, themselves lying flatte prostrate, and so to chaunte out their lessons by peece-meale, being the most part lustie fellows of twenty-five years and upwards.'

Giraldus Cambrensis noted that he had 'never seen among any other people so many blind by birth, so many lame, so many maimed in body and so many suffering from some natural defect'. Typically he attributed the facts on which he based this observation (which like many other of his observations may not be accurate) to sexual liberty among the Irish. Yet the Irish were not sexually depraved as the Normans thought, although the Normans may well have been misled in good faith because the legal toleration of concubinage among the Irish contrasted with the strict marriage conventions of the Normans, and shocked them by suggesting a still wider freedom of morals. The Normans had difficulty in appreciating the relative absence of conventional restraints in Irish society. This was apparent also in Giraldus' assessment of the bringing up of young children in a largely unsupervised manner: 'when they are born they are not carefully nursed as is usual. For

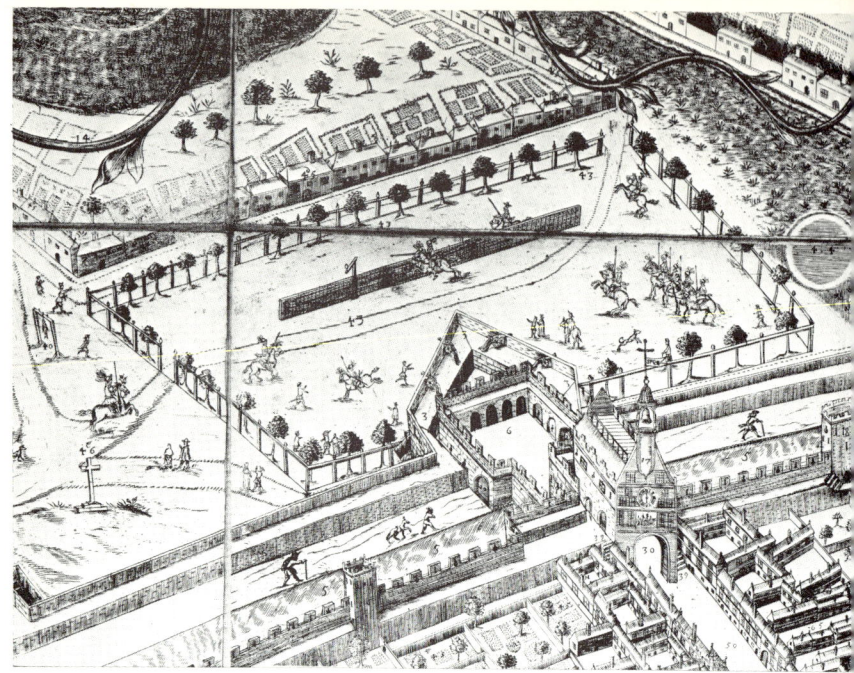

Tilting

apart from the nourishment with which they are sustained by their hard parents from dying altogether, they are for the rest abandoned to ruthless nature.' Similarly the free and easy manners of the grown Irish and the absence of strict conventions of decorum shocked even a person such as the English squire, Henry Castide, who had lived for many years among the Irish and had married the daughter of an Irishman: 'these kings were of coarse manners and understanding and in spite of all that I could do to soften their language and nature, very little progress has been made, for they would frequently return to their former coarse behaviour.'

The table manners of the Irish also seemed to leave much to be desired, but it was not only their manners that shocked the Normans but the fact that Irish rulers, in allowing their retainers to join them at table, contradicted the deeply ingrained Norman sense of social cleavage between lord and retainers. 'I observed', said Henry Castide of the four Irish kings, whom he was preparing for knighthood in Dublin in 1399, 'that, as they sat at table, they made grimaces, and I resolved in my own mind to make them drop that custom. When these kings were seated at table, and the first dish was served, they would make their minstrels and principal servants sit beside them, eat from their plates, and drink from their cups. They told me this was a praiseworthy custom in their country, where everything was in common but their bed.'

Yet with all their faults, real or imagined, the Irish had many good points: in particular they were warm in their friendship. Henry Castide's captor, an Irishman, Bryan Costeret, gave him his daughter in marriage, and was prepared to give him his liberty again only 'provided my eldest daughter remained with him. I returned to England and fixed residence at Bristol. My two children are married—the one in Ireland has three boys and two girls, and her sister four boys and two daughters.' In Tudor times Borde accused the Irish of being 'angry and testy without a cause'. But this was a common fault among the Normans or English themselves in Ireland. Easy provocation to anger and senseless violence or killing abounded.

Music was very popular among the Irish. Giraldus Cambrensis conceded that 'it is only in the case of musical instruments that I find any commendable diligence in this people'.

Soldiers wading into the sea to unload provisions

An Irish chieftain feasting

Statutory attempts to prohibit the employment of Irish musicians among the Normans were of no avail, and violation of the Statutes was connived at by the authorities themselves. In 1376 the Parliament of the lordship got permission to enact that 'Donal O'Moghane, Irish minstrel, may dwell among the English and be in their houses'. One of the most common sports was hurling, and it was more on account of the maiming of the able-bodied in hurling than its Irish origin that the Parliament enacted that 'the commons of the land of Ireland, who are in divers marches of war, use not henceforth the games which are called hurling, with great clubs and ball upon the ground, from which great evils and maims have arisen'. Play with weapons was also common. Among the Irish 'a young knight begins to learn to tilt with a light lance, against a shield fixed in a post in a field, and the more lances he breaks, the more honour he acquires'.

Much time was also spent in taverns, although as in Galway in 1585, where the taverns were 'not in any honest sorte keapte cleane, wherein ther is neither sitting-place, clothe, dish or any other service', they must have been very sparse and austere in their furnishings and appearance. Women also frequented the taverns: in 1302 John Le Foulere by driving his horse deliberately into a tavern injured Felicia, daughter of John, 'when Felicia was drinking in a tavern amongst others in the town of

CONFLICT IN IRELAND: OLD ORDER AND NEW TOWNS

Tamehager'. A picture of how a number of men might spend a day is presented in a case which came before the Justiciar's Court in 1311, because it ended in a killing. The background to the incident involved a number of men 'playing in a meadow near Leghlyn and [who] threw their lances there, and afterwards towards evening they came to Leghlyn and drank wine there in an inn, and shortly afterwards quarrelled as to who should pay for the drink'. Wine was very common, although ale was cheaper and among the ordinary people the better-known beverage. Whiskey or aqua vitae was distilled by the Irish. Sir John Perrott in the sixteenth century noted that it might 'rather to be cald aqua mortis to poyson the people, than comfort them in any good sorte'.

The spectre of hunger or want was never far removed even from the lives of many that by the standards of the time must be regarded as comparatively well-to-do, although the movement of grain supplies within the country helped to prevent shortages. An extensive foreign trade in grain developed in the Norman ports; in years of good harvests grain was exported, and when the harvest failed want was relieved by imports. But despite the growth of trade the consequences of poor harvests could still on occasion be very severe. The Annals of Innisfallen state of one of the years of the thirteenth century, for instance, that 'there was a great famine in the same year so that multitudes of poor people died of cold and hunger and the rich suffered hardship'. Even in the towns there was much poverty. Creton's description of his arrival in Waterford with Richard's expedition in 1399 suggests that even to the contemporary visitor the impression of poor living conditions and of a primitive organization of work was striking: 'In less than two days we came in sight of the Tower of Waterford, in Ireland: where the wretched and filthy people, some in rags, others girt with a rope, had the one a hole, the other a hut for their dwelling. These were forced to carry great burdens, and to go into the water up to their waists, for the speedy unloading of the barges from the sea.'

For many people life was not only simple, but primitive. Borde, a Tudor visitor, stated that among the Irish 'in many

Irish chieftain in full dress

places they care not for pot, pan, kettil, nor for mattrys, fether bed, nor such implements of houshold'. A consequence of the fewness of pots was the survival of methods of cooking which were age-old: 'in those partyes they will eate theyr meat sytting on the ground or erth. And they wyl sethe theyr meat in a beastes skin. And the skyn shall be set in manye stakes of wood, and than they wyll put in the water and the fleshe and than they wyl make a great fyre under the skyn betwixt the stakes and the skyne wyl not greatly bren. And whan the meate is eaten, they for theyr drynke, wil drinke up the brothe.' But scarcity of utensils was not confined to the Irish. Under the will of Hugh Brady, Bishop of Meath, in 1583, the poor inhabitants of Dunboyne were given the use of his best pan amongst them 'to serve their turns' and the Portrieve of the town was to settle any controversy as to borrowing or keeping the pan too long.

Even among the farmers in the Pale utensils and furniture must have been modest and simple, and must have contrasted sharply with items such as 'a white bed with three curtains', 'two tables for cups called cupboards', and 'five bankers with five cushions', mentioned in the wills of the very well-to-do.

Head of an Irish chieftain, Turloch Luineach O'Neill, 1575

There was considerable contrast in dress between Norman and Irish, although by the sixteenth century Irish rulers rivalled English lords in the opulence of their dress, albeit in different style. Originally Irish dress had consisted of a smock or shirt made of linen and of a mantle of wool with an edge of shaggy material. Norman dress was more elaborate, although many adopted in particular the Irish mantle or 'falling'. The clothes taken from a murdered man in 1305 included a 'falling' worth 18*d*, a tunic worth 12*d*, a hood (3*d*), breeches (4*d*), a pair of shoes (2*d*), a spear (6*d*) and a belt with knife and purse (4*d*), the purse containing 2*s* in silver. A striking contrast between the dress of the two races at this time was the absence of anything approximating to breeches among the Irish. Henry Castide stated that: 'they had another custom which I knew to be common in that country, which was the not wearing breeches. I had in consequence, plenty of breeches made of linen and cloth, which I gave to the kings and their attendants, and accustomed them to wear them.'

Irish dress changed in the course of the following centuries. Skin-tight trews, stitched at the back, known among the Irish but little used, had become common features of dress by the sixteenth century. At the same time the smock or tunic no longer reached to the ankles: it also acquired an opening at the front, and the sleeves became baggy. A jacket reaching no further than the hips also came into use, being worn over the tunic or in some instances replacing it. Many of the ordinary Irish, however, continued to wear neither trews nor shoes, being thus bare-footed and bare-legged. English dress continued to contrast with the evolving Irish dress. Henry VIII's Ordinances to the town of Galway in 1536 required the inhabitants not to wear mantles in the street as the Irish did, but rather cloaks or gowns, coats, doublets and hose after the English manner. A by-law of the Guild Merchant in Dublin in 1573 regulating dress 'such as becometh a prentize' gives a good impression of contemporary male dress: 'a coate of clothe decentely made without gardinge cuttinge or sylke to be wroght thereon', 'a doublet of sm thinge', 'a shurte of this cowntrey clothe with a decente band theirrto of the leikke clothe and the ruff thearof to be one yard longe', 'a payre of hose whiche shall not be made of any more clothe than towe [i.e. two] yardes being yarde broade', 'the breche of the same hose shall not be bolsterede out with ether wool, heyre or eny other thinge but shalbe with one lyininge wch shalbe close to the tieghe'.

Within these centuries many important changes had taken place in Ireland. The assimilation of two different races had made some progress. The towns were no longer an exotic feature, but, apart from the fact that they had been drawn only to a limited extent into the cultural assimilation afoot in rural Ireland, were fairly well integrated into an economy in which both internal and foreign trade were much more important than in the past. Moreover, despite the rural character of most of the country and the remoteness of Ireland from the main stream of European culture, the influence of the spirit of the Renaissance was evident in Ireland and among the Irish no less than among the English. The Book of Lismore, written around 1500 for Finghin MacCarthy Reagh, contained a translation of the travels of Marco Polo. The library of the ninth Earl of Kildare contained 112 parchment books, a considerable number for the days before printing: 34 in Latin, 36 in French, 22 in English and 20 in Irish. A notable lack in Irish education had been the want of a university. As a result many in Ireland had to go to Oxford, including not only the King's subjects but 'wylde Irishmen' whose 'malice and misdeeds continue from day to day to the great slander of the said University'. Ireland, despite its racial divisions, had by no means stood aside from the economic and cultural changes of the age.

Further Reading

J. F. M. Lydon, 'The problem of the frontier in medieval Ireland', in *Studies in Irish history, Topic*, no. 13, Spring 1967, Washington and Jefferson College, Washington, Pa.
G. Mac Niocaill, *Na buirgéisí*, vol. 2, 1964
T. W. Moody and F. X. Martin (ed.), *The course of Irish history*, 1967
B. O'Cuiv (ed.), *Seven centuries of Irish learning*, 1000–1700, 1961
J. J. O'Meara (ed.), *The topography of Ireland by Giraldus Cambrensis*, 1951
M. D. O'Sullivan, *Old Galway*, 1942
J. Otway-Ruthven, 'The organisation of Anglo-Irish agriculture in the middle ages', in *Journal of the Royal Society of Antiquaries of Ireland*, vol. LXXXI, pt. 1, 1951
D. B. Quinn, *The Elizabethans and the Irish*, 1966
J. J. Webb, *The guilds of Dublin*, 1918
J. F. M. Lydon, *The lordship of Ireland in the middle ages*, 1972
—— *Ireland in the later middle ages*, 1973

III

A Period of Change
1550-1700

Despite changes Ireland was still a medieval country in the mid-sixteenth century. The towns had not outgrown the areas enclosed by their century-old walls nor had the inhabitants abandoned their intensely local outlook. But within the next century and a half much of the old was to disappear. The country in 1700 was more densely populated than it had ever been; with a rapid growth of trade the towns were outgrowing their mental and physical isolation; the transition from medieval to modern was evident in the lives of town-dwellers and more modestly in the lives of most countrymen.

Despite a loss of many lives in the wars, and in the plagues and famines that followed the wars, of the late sixteenth and seventeenth centuries, the long-term trend was for a substantial rise in population. As early as the 1680s the population may have exceeded two millions. A denser population had considerable consequences for agriculture. More extensive settlement was incompatible with such old customs as *creaghting* or the migration of cattle from winter to summer pastures, a practice which declined rapidly in the seventeenth century. There were further inroads on the forests. In addition the growing demand for charcoal for the iron-smelting furnaces, multiplying in response to the expansion of the market for iron, quickened the felling of the woodlands. The lairs of the wolves became fewer and fewer: the last wolf in co. Cork is said to have been killed in 1710.

Milking a cow

Changes in agriculture were themselves in part a response to the striking growth in trade in this period. Within the medieval period trade in agricultural products had been confined to a small number of products such as skins, hides and wool. Trade in grain was important only when harvests proved inadequate or when a surplus arising from a bumper crop was disposed of as opportunity offered. In the seventeenth century, however, agricultural exports, stimulated by a rising market in England, increased rapidly. Exports in 1665 were larger than in 1641; in 1698 they were larger than in 1665. In other words agriculture was increasingly market-orientated. Sheep, cattle and wool were the main exports. Even the Cattle Acts prohibiting the import of cattle and sheep from Ireland to England in the 1660s had only a limited impact on the upsurge of the country's foreign trade: movements in relative prices would have, even without the Cattle Acts, ensured a swing-away from the shipment of live cattle and sheep to dairying for the continental butter market and to wool for the English market.

Agricultural practices themselves also tended to change for

the better. Primitive methods such as ploughing by the tail or burning grain in the straw, frequently deplored by contemporaries, were disappearing in many parts of the country. Some commentators even spoke favourably of Irish agricultural practice. Vincent Gookin in 1655 noted that 'there are few of the Irish commonalty but are skilful in husbandry and more exact than any English in the husbandry proper to that country'. Nor was tillage neglected. Most areas produced enough grain for their own needs, and where markets were at hand, were able to produce a surplus to supply them. Of Kildare, for instance, a contemporary wrote in 1683 that 'the painful husbandman' was encouraged 'to turn all under the plough, and Dublin being in the neighbourhood ever does afford them a good market'. The fact that the open-field system, where it had been established at all, was breaking down even before 1500 in many places may have added to the flexibility of Irish agriculture. The wholesale transfer by successive confiscations after the wars of the sixteenth and seventeenth centuries of most of the land into the hands of English and Scottish settlers helped further to free Irish agriculture from any communal limitation on land use. As a result Irish agriculture responded rather readily to shifting market possibilities in the seventeenth and eighteenth centuries.

The pervasive growth of trade was reflected in a significant growth of new wealth and in the consumption of new or exotic products. Though the consumption of tobacco, introduced to Europe only in the sixteenth century, was still modest in the early seventeenth century, it soared subsequently. Imports exceeded a million pounds in 1665 and three million

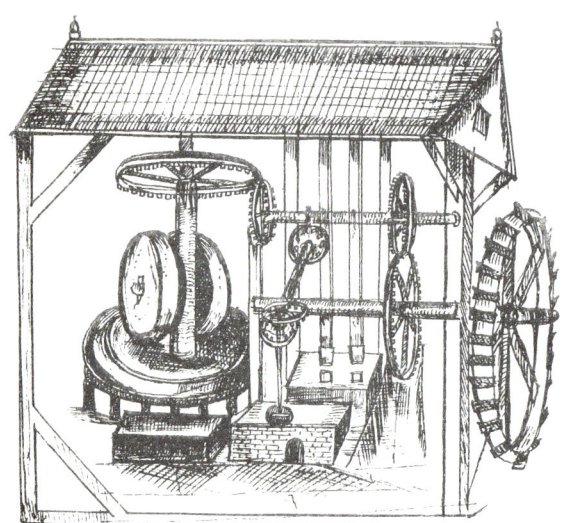

Machinery of a water-mill

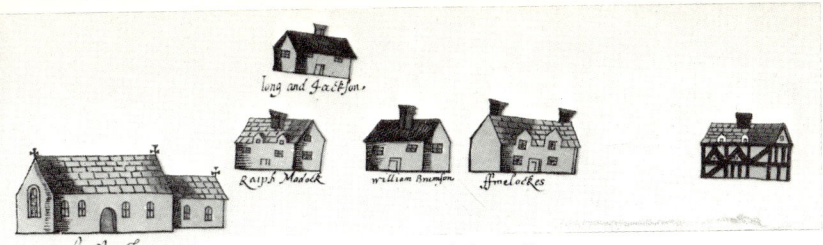

Settlers' houses and church in co. Derry

pounds in the early 1680s. Sir William Petty commented on how widespread tobacco-smoking was among the ordinary people. Women no less than men smoked. Dunton, an English visitor of the 1690s, related how 'the elder people sit spectators telling stories of their own like feats in days of yore, and now and then divert themselves with a quill full of sneezing or a whiff of tobacco; for one short foul pipe of an inch long, the shorter and fouler the better, will serve a dozen of them men and women together, the first holding the smoke in his mouth until everyone has whiffed once or twice, and when the pipe returns to him he blows it out of his nose.'

The growth of trade was accompanied by a remarkable increase in travel and by a gradual improvement in communications. Sir George Rawdon, for instance, in the Restoration period mentions a visit to Mullingar fair from his home in Lisburn, though 120 miles distant, as nothing out of the ordinary. Shops were still few, and to be found only in the towns. In consequence pedlars and chapmen were necessarily important in the distribution of goods. But not only were their services vital, but in an age when even at the very end of the century Dublin was alone among Irish towns in having a newspaper, the pedlars, sleeping in the cabins of peasants along their route, played an invaluable part in bringing into remote areas news of the world beyond.

Windmill outside the town of Youghal

'An Inn for Travailers'

Travel itself was still far from easy, though it was of course the increased amount of travel by contemporaries that brought to light the tribulations of the traveller. Although bridges replaced many of the fords at which it had not been uncommon for lives to be lost, the condition of the roads themselves, especially during the bad weather of the winter months, remained appalling. As John Stevens noted of the country near Drogheda: 'the great rain has made the ways almost impassable, the horse road which is most old cause way being broken up and quite out of repair and the footway in the fields very boggy with abundance of ditches at that time full of water. In such conditions people still commonly travelled on horseback, and goods were carried by pack-horse.

However, roads were being improved. As a result the use of

A ferry carrying men and a horse across the Foyle at Derry

House and fort at Omagh

carriages by the well-to-do increased. The first stage-coaches also made their appearance. Dunton in describing a trip from Dublin to Drogheda mentioned Ballough, 'a very poor sorry town with an inn where the stage-coach to Drogheda sets in at noon'. A measure of the increase in travel was the inns on the main roads from the capital. Improved communications were vital to the satisfaction of the traveller's curiosity: the number of foreign visitors who left an account of their itineraries in Ireland in the seventeenth century is a reminder that the tourist's curiosity and greater facilities for travel went hand in hand. The establishment of a public post contributed also to the improvement in communications, facilitating commerce and the rapid transmission of correspondence. Mental isolation no less than physical isolation was breaking down. The post for Cork from Dublin, for instance, carried on horseback by post-boys, set out twice a week on Tuesdays and Saturdays.

The development of trade and communications was made easier by peaceful conditions. From the beginning of the seventeenth century the King's Peace was for the first time effective

A PERIOD OF CHANGE 1550-1700

throughout the island, and was seriously disturbed only during the great political and military upheavals of the 1640s and early 1650s and 1689-91. The maintenance of bands of armed retainers for purposes of private warfare, once common even in loyal areas, was no longer usual. Many families still lived in the castellated houses of medieval times, with their adjoining *bawn* or walled enclosure, and such houses were still being built in the seventeenth century. Even in the second half of the century the houses of most gentlemen in the barony of Forth in Wexford were 'fortified with castles of quadrangle form, some 60 feet high with walls five feet thick'.

However, new and more spacious houses in which the preoccupation with defence was less, began to be built even as far back as Tudor times. Their rooms were more spacious and were lighted by large windows even on the ground floor. The manor-house built at Carrick by the tenth Earl of Ormonde is an early example. Even if the walled enclosure was also built, new houses were often lighter and less forbidding. Existing castellated houses often had an annexe with additional living-quarters added on to them. Rathcline House in co. Longford, belonging to the second Viscount Lanesborough, contained a Damask room, a dining-room, two drawing-rooms, My Lord's dressing-room, parlour, parlour closet, Castle room and room adjoining, My Lady's closet, Red room, room above Damask room, Madame Lane's room and room adjoining, the Nurseries, the Lobby, butler's garret, cook's garret, and four other garrets. In the second half of the century Clarendon remarked that 'within little more than two years . . . were many buildings raised for beauty as well as use, orderly and regular plantations of trees and fences and enclosures raised throughout the kingdom.'

Despite more peaceful conditions there was still, however, an

The Duke of Ormonde's house at Kilkenny from the Bridge

An Irish nobleman and his wife

abiding element of insecurity. The inventory of Rathcline House bore witness to an imposing array of weapons in 1688: '20 pikes, 12 fire-locks, 5 carabines, 4 blunderbusses, 1 fuzee, 3 long fowling pieces'. This lingering feeling of insecurity was, however, occasioned not by private warfare but by the presence of bands of rapparees or tories. The appearance of such bands was in part due to the pickings which the increase in trade and in passenger traffic on the roads offered. Tories such as Redmond O'Hanlon haunted the routes between the north and Dublin in the desolate lands above Dundalk. The tories were frequently 'the offspring of gentlemen that have either misspent or forfeited their estates who, though having no subsistence, yet condemn and despise trades as being too mean and base for a gentleman reduced ever so low'. Political motives sometimes served to cover their actions, the tories being encouraged 'by their priests and followers in an opinion that they may yet recover their lands and live in their predecessors splendour'. Yet robbery with violence on the highway or elsewhere did not appear that prevalent to the contemporary: according to a description of co. Kildare in 1683 'the robberies, felonies, burglaries, etc., usually committed in this kingdom are not so numerous but there are commonly sentenced to die in a monthly sessions at the Old Bailey more than in a half-year's circuit of Ireland'. In essence the rapparees were the last flowering of a tradition of lawlessness that the medieval administration had never been able to suppress.

Change in their surroundings was evident even to contemporaries. They frequently related these changes to the great social and political revolution that engulfed Ireland between 1550 and 1700. During the Reformation in the sixteenth century the Anglo-Normans like the Irish had remained faithful to the old religion and in the ensuing political and religious conflict they, as well as the Irish, lost their lands through confiscation and redistribution to new settlers from England and Scotland. To the dispossessed families and their immediate retainers, the general changes of the age by association with the revolution in landownership appeared to be for the worst. Indeed the revolution appeared to be the cause of all change. Even the destruction of the woods was seen not as an inevitable economic change but as a direct consequence of the changes in landownership. A seventeenth-century poet bewailed their destruction:

> *What shall we henceforth do without timber,*
> *the last of the woods is fallen.*

Another Gaelic poet declared:

> *Now the wood is being cut,*
> *We will journey over the sea.*

The deep pathos in such poems was occasioned not by the cutting down of woodlands but by the decay of a familiar social order. What the poets bewailed was the passing of the medieval hospitality of the old houses, and the thing most resented in the new settlers was their indifference to these traditions and to the professional Gaelic poet who had a welcome place at the entertainments of the old order.

The poets were blind to the inevitability of social and economic change. Even without the revolution they lamented, the growth of markets for timber, livestock and grain inevitably led landowners to develop a commercial attitude and acquisitiveness that would have made little sense in a more static world where trade was limited and wealth was enumerated in kind and in the maintenance of retainers rather than in cash. The voice of writers such as O'Bruadair, who complained that poets were no longer esteemed as they had been, is in fact the last articulate protest at the passing of medieval society. The cutting down of the woods, given its financial attractiveness,

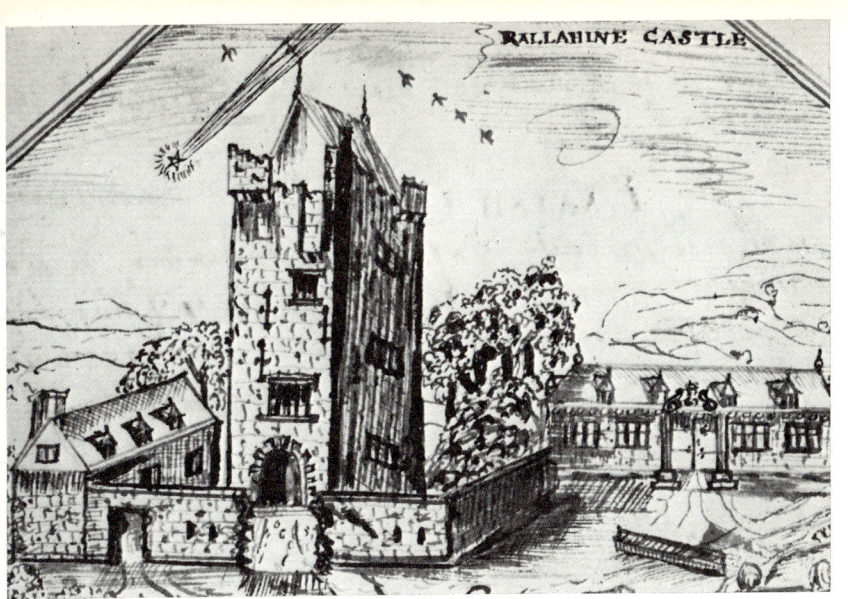
Stables built at Rallahine Castle, co. Clare

was inevitable, and the growth of population and of markets for the products of the soil meant that rather little land would revert to forest. But so keen was the financial sense of contemporaries that there were already some who could see that reafforestation could pay. Lord Massareene in the north went so far as to say that his 'greatest entertainment is planting'. Contemporaries were also quick to see that horse-racing, which was now becoming very popular, offered profits in breeding horses as well as diversion. Writing in 1670 from co. Clare, Colonel Daniel O'Brien remarked: 'I begin to be the greatest breeder of horses in the King's dominions for I keep about my house 16,000 acres for my mares, colts and deer.'

In the old order that was passing away, the dependence of tenants, Anglo-Irish as well as Irish, on their lord was great. A statement as late as 1674 that 'the commonalty are extremely awed by their superiors, in such sort, a tenant fears as much to speak against a lord of the manor, or their next powerful neighbour, as wise men would dread to speak treason against a prince under whose allegiance he lives and hath sworn to' has a medieval ring. The downfall of the old order did not of itself add to the oppression of the ordinary man, and he can not have seen its passing with the same nostalgia as the Gaelic poets,

A PERIOD OF CHANGE 1550-1700

who shared the social outlook of their masters. The poets despised the ordinary people and were indifferent to their lot. In O'Bruadair's case the fact that through force of circumstances he was reduced to work as a labourer in no way softened his attitude towards the common people. In many ways the ordinary people stood to gain by the return of settled conditions after the wars and by the growth of trade, which favoured the development of an orderly commercial relationship between tenant and landlord in place of the often arbitrary one that had prevailed especially in unsettled conditions.

The diet of the well-to-do was of course comparatively varied. But the diet of the common people, except for the very poorest, was far from being confined to the potato. An account of Kildare in 1683 describes the diet of the people as 'very mean and sparing, consisting of milk, roots and coarse unsavoury bread'. Fifteen years later Dunton, after referring to cabins of the lowest order in the same county, related how 'behind one of their cabins lies the garden, a piece of ground sometimes of half an acre, and in this is the turf stack, their corn, perhaps 200 to 300 sheaves of oats and as much peas. The rest of the ground is full of their dearly beloved potatoes, and a few cabbages which the solitary calf of the family that is here part from its dam never suffers to come to perfection.' Oaten bread was common. In a poor cabin in Iar-Connacht, Dunton was offered for supper oaten cakes along with 'a greate roll of fresh butter of three pounds at least, and a wodden vessell full of milk and water' and a 'hare swimming in a wodden boul full of oyl of butter'. It was the sparsity of meat in the diet that made the most striking contrast with the diet of the well-to-do. In the home of 'one O'Flaghertie the most considerable man in this territorye', supper was much the same as the previous night in the poor cabin, 'only there was a mutton killed for supper, half of which was boyld and the other roasted, and all devour'd at the meale'. At dinner the next day was served 'no less than a whole beef boyl'd and roasted, and what mutton I know not so profewsly did they lay it on the table. At the upper end where the lady sate was placed an heap of oaten cakes above a foot high, such another in the middle and the like at the lower end.'

Housing for the ordinary people was bad. But bad housing for many denoted the survival of traditional standards rather than poverty. At their worst the cabins were made 'by laying one end of the stick upon the bank of a ditch, and the other upon a little bit of a mud wall and then when it is wattled they cover it with heath, straw or scraws of earth, and into this miserable place will half a dozen poor creatures creep for shelter and lodging'. Houses were generally

Irish cabins outside the Fort of Monaghan

better than this. But chimneys were only beginning to become commonplace. Even O'Flaghertie, visited by Dunton, was living in a habitation with 'no chimney but a vent hole for the smoake at the ridge, and I observ'd the people here much troubled with sore eyes', and excused the disagreeable circumstances only by saying that 'they had newly put up this for a booley or summer habitation, the proper dwelling or mansion house being some miles farther neare the sea'. Petty, however, estimated one-fifth of the houses to have a chimney. Dunton himself reported coming on 'a contemptible habitation' of 'a little Irish town of about nine cabins with two chimneys each' in the north of co. Dublin. Houses of stone were also becoming more common in parts of the country where traditional modes of house-building were meeting outside influences. Gookin, in saying in 1655 that for every 100 men there were five or six carpenters and masons among the Irish, 'and these more handy and ready in building ordinary houses, and much more prudent in supplying the defects of instruments and materials, than English artificers', was probably speaking the truth as far as many of the more advanced parts of the country were concerned.

Living conditions were still primitive. Even among the upper classes hygiene was not greatly attended to. In a detailed inventory of household goods in Castlemartyr in 1677 the only bath mentioned was a 'bathing tub' stowed away with broken furniture. For all save the very well-to-do bedding was simple: 'in the better sort of cabins there is commonly one flock bed, seldom more, feathers being too costly; this serves the man and his wife, the rest all lie on straw, some with one sheet and blanket, others only their clothes and blanket to cover them.' The floor was generally an earthen one, and, following medieval practice, was often covered with rushes. Simplicity and fewness of household goods may be explained by the fact that, until the Industrial Revolution cheapened them in the eighteenth century, they were beyond the reach of most people, and not only of the very poor.

The traditions associated with the old schools of medicine survived in many parts of the country. Qualified medical men were, however, few, and to be found only in the towns. Despite their fewness, they do not appear to have been overworked by modern standards. Dr Thomas Arthur, one of the best-known medical men of the second half of the century, seldom saw more than one patient a day. Much of their time was moreover taken up in prolonged absences to care for titled patients. In 1684, for instance, a Dr Morris received £40 for constant attendance during a period of five weeks on Lady Inchiquin, 'never leaving the house'.

The pastimes and leisure occupations of the well-to-do were changing rapidly in the seventeenth century. In particular horse-racing was coming to the fore. On the Curragh there were already by the end of the seventeenth century 'several fine horses kept hereabouts for the race in stables built on purpose'. While the old-style gregarious entertainments were declining, new and more individual interests were developing. Books were cheaper and more readily available. The fact that Dunton, a London

Village of Staplestown, co. Carlow

A PERIOD OF CHANGE 1550-1700

bookseller, came to Dublin to do business is itself a testimony to the growth of a market for books. A minority of landed and professional gentlemen devoted their time to philosophic speculation and scientific experiment, and came together to discuss their interests.

Among the ordinary people the interest in music and dancing remained as strong as ever. Dunton related how in co. Kildare 'after the matrimonial ceremony was over we had a bag piper and a blind harper that dinned us with their music, to which there was perpetual dancing'. Wakes no less than weddings were social occasions. An account of Kildare in 1683 referred to 'their wakes also over dead corpses, where they have a table spread and served with the best that can be had at such a time, and after a while attending ... they fall to eating and drinking, after to revelling, as if one of the feasts of Bacchus'. The keening of the dead person by his friends and relatives was a feature of the burials. Professional assistance was common in this work: 'if there be not enough to make out a good cry they hire the best and deepest mouthed in all the country and so they proceed towards the church'. The keeners also partook of the refreshment. Dunton related how before a funeral he saw 'about 20 women guzzling usqubagh or aqua viate; I enquired who they were, and was told they were the *mna keena* or howling

Five men doing a sword-dance

Galway in 1685

women, who had this given them to support their spirits in that laborious work'.

Hurling matches often attracted crowds. The indefatigable Dunton related how 'you may sometimes see one of the gamesters carry the ball tossing it for 40 or 50 yards in spite of all the adverse players; and when he is like to lose it, he generally gives it a great stroke to drive it towards the goal.' The game, according to Dunton, was played between goals 200 to 300 yards apart, in the presence of as many as 2,000 spectators. 'At this sport one parish sometimes or barony challenges another; they pick out 10, 12 or 20 players of a side, and the prize is generally a barrel or two of ale, which is brought into the field and drunk by the victors on the spot, though the vanquished are not without a share of it too.' As for playing football, according to the same source, 'only in a small territory called Fingal near Dublin people use it much, and trip, and shoulder very handsomely'.

The towns still retained their walls in the seventeenth century, and because of the military campaigns of the period even added to their fortifications. In the early decades the planters of the north and north-east laid out their towns within circuits of wall. But as the century advanced the suburbs outside the walls grew rapidly. Moreover, life within the walls was losing its medieval character. Although the guilds existed, their regulations were ceasing to be effective, and did not apply at all to the growing industrial population in the suburbs. Soon the cities were to lose their walls altogether. This was already foreshadowed in Dublin at the end of the seventeenth century with the demolition in 1698 of the Dams Gate near the Castle. In the suburbs many of the houses were simply thatched

A PERIOD OF CHANGE 1550–1700

cabins. Within the walls, however, most of the houses were substantial, and in Galway in particular many of the houses were of stone. Timber houses were in most towns more common than stone. In the Corn Market in Dublin, there were, for instance, 'large timber houses, on the ground floor kitchen and one lodging room, second and third three rooms each, and fourth two garrets'.

By no means all the towns presented a prosperous appearance. Where towns were centres of trade or on busy routes, they did well. Drogheda, according to Dunton, 'is a handsome, clean, English-like town, and the best I have seen in Ireland except the metropolis'. Towns which were not on trade routes, unless they happened to be assize towns, had little traffic. Kildare, for instance, 'is but a poor place, not lying in any road, and not having any trade belonging to it. There are some shops with hops, iron, salt and tobacco, and the merchant not worth 40 pound.' Within a great expanse of medieval walls, Athenry was 'a poor pitiful miserable place, full of cabins and several ruined stone houses and castles'.

An ancient wooden house

Dublin more than any other town gained from the growth of trade and from the greater power of government in the seventeenth century. Brereton in 1635 stated that 'this city of Dublin is extending his bounds and limits very far; much additions of buildings lately, and some of them very fair, stately and complete buildings. . . . Here are divers commodities cried in Dublin as in London which it doth more resemble than any town I have ever seen in the King of England's dominions.' The French traveller, Jorevin de Rocheford,

Street scene in Cork, c. 1630

in 1668 thought Dublin 'one of the greatest and best peopled cities in Europe'. In the second half of the century Dublin may have had a population of around 40,000 and was already beginning to spread far beyond its medieval walls. Its expansion led to building on the northern side of the Liffey. From one before 1670 the number of bridges in the city had increased to four by the end of the century. Development reached out on the south side as far as the site where St Stephen's Green was laid out by the Corporation, and, in the south-west, the already extensive industrial suburb of the Liberties, 'a large and spacious one able to furnish out some thousands of brawny weavers and other tradesmen of good reputation and substance, for the greatest part of the woollen trade wrought in Dublin is here, and a large handsome street called the Coom has little in it more than clothiers' shops and weavers' houses'. This district was enriched by an inflow of French Huguenot craftsmen and after 1690 Dutch and Flemings, who were responsible for introducing the fashion of building in brick. The houses they introduced were known as Dutch Billies with the roof-ridge at right angles to the street.

Though the streets of central Dublin were the same tortuous ones of medieval times and though they were flanked with houses built as far back as the reign of Elizabeth and earlier, they now carried a much greater traffic: 'the streets are much pestered with hucksters sitting under bulks and stalls in the streets whereby the streets are made so narrow that coaches or carts cannot well pass or turn.' This congestion was especially serious because at this time wheeled traffic was multiplying. In addition to private carriages, horse-drawn hackney cars already plied: in 1687 there were 80 licensed hackneys on the hazards in addition to a number of pirates. A profusion of ale-houses and taverns, the coming into vogue of the coffee-houses, and the building of a theatre at Smock Alley tempted people out of doors at night. With plenty of animation in the streets in contrast with the calm following curfew in the medieval period, some attempt at dispelling darkness in the streets was necessary. In 1687 the first public lighting was provided: lanterns and candles were hung out from selected houses every night in the winter from 5 to 10 'for the prevention of many mischiefs and inconveniences in the streets in the dark nights'. In a sense street lighting in Dublin, as much as the felling of the woods in the countryside, marked the death of the medieval world.

A Ringsend coach

Old house in Marrowbone Lane, Dublin

Further Reading

M. Craig, *Dublin, 1660–1860, a social and architectural history*, 1952
J. Carty, *Ireland from the Flight of the Earls to Grattan's Parliament (1607–1782)*, 1949
E. MacLysaght, *Irish life in the seventeenth century*, 1950
C. Maxwell, *The stranger in Ireland*, 1954
D. F. Moore, *Dublin*, 1965
Sir William Petty, *Economic writings* (ed. C. H. Hull) (2 vols), 1899
D. B. Quinn, *The Elizabethans and the Irish*, 1966
T. C. Barnard, *Cromwellian Ireland: English government and reform in Ireland, 1649–1660*, 1975
N. P. Canny, *The Elizabethan Conquest of Ireland*, 1976
L. M. Cullen, 'Population trends in seventeenth-century Ireland', *Economic and social review*, vol. vi (1975)
T. W. Moody, F. X. Martin, F. J. Byrne (eds), *A new history of Ireland*, vol. iii, *1534–1691*, 1976

IV

Town and Country in the Eighteenth Century

Dublin in the eighteenth century bore little resemblance to the essentially medieval city of a century previously, and its more far-reaching role in Irish economic and social life testified to the fact that change had also affected much of the rest of the country. But at the outset there were still areas in which, because of their physical isolation, much of the older social order and way of life survived. Even the new planter families in remote areas succumbed readily to the influences of a social order which was in many ways more a survival of medieval life than something especially Irish. Where planter families conformed to the old way of life and to its traditions of hospitality, the Irish poets were prepared to express their warm appreciation of the hospitality they received. Egan O'Rahilly, a bitter critic of the changes in Cork and Kerry, praised without reserve the hospitality of the planter, Warner, in whose house there was:

> Meat on spits, and wild fowl from the ocean;
> Music and song, and drinking bouts;
> Delicious roast beef and spotless honey,
> Hounds and dogs and baying.

Another Gaelic poet, Seán Clárach O'Domhnaill, though less in touch with the medieval past than O'Rahilly, described in appreciative terms the household of Thomas Greene of Gort an Tóchair, co. Clare:

The Kilruddery Hunt, co. Wicklow

Drinking, gambling, violins,
The sweetness of gentle song in tune,
A crowd uproariously drunk,
And a band eager for merriment.

While the old way of life was strong enough in places to resist the upheaval in landownership, its breakdown was inevitable. With the King's Peace already effective, the pursuit of arms and the maintenance of bands of followers sharing profusely in their chief's food, drink and entertainment, was no longer necessary. But in areas where trade was little developed and where there was little outlet for surplus output, the hospitality itself did not appear wasteful, and the old traditions declined only slowly. The growth of trade in the course of the seventeenth century offered new prospects of commercial gain, and led to a growing interest in estate management in areas strongly affected by change. Even outside the more remote areas, many of the gentry were barely literate; much of their time was spent out of doors in hunting and at other times was frittered away in drinking. Crude living habits were common and acceptable in society. But already there was growing evidence of change in outlook and behaviour. In the following century there was a general softening of manners and a greater emphasis on the social graces. Intellectual interests were also more commonplace. Much behaviour that would not have merited comment a century previously was now looked on askance.

TOWN AND COUNTRY IN THE EIGHTEENTH CENTURY

Changes in social life came last in areas which were remote and where trade and contact with the outside world had been limited. In such districts landed families were still patriarchal, receiving payment in kind from their tenants and dispensing hospitality in the old manner. But even in such areas commercial attitudes made an appearance. Paradoxically the subsistence condition of such areas itself quickened the process of change. Where trade did not exist, landed families, often faced with a glut of goods from their tenants, were forced to seek market outlets, and in doing so to develop their commercial sense. Some families entered directly into foreign trade and into the ownership of shipping on their own account or in conjunction with merchants from the towns. In time, as trade reached into these areas, the direct interest of landed families in such business ventures declined, but a more acute commercial sense survived. Cash circulated more freely, and the payment of rents in cash in place of kind furthered the change. With the growth of trade and a freer circulation of money, life even for the ordinary people was enriched by the appearance of new goods. The Rosses in co. Donegal as described by a gentleman in the 1750s were a simple subsistence community where the sole luxuries were tobacco and spirits, and rents were paid in kind, but when he visited the area again in 1787 he saw 'spruce young lads fashionably dressed on Sundays in satin waistcoats and breeches, with white silk stockings, silken buckles and ruffled shirts'.

The main economic feature of the age was the expansion of trade. Inland, the development of an elaborate network of markets and fairs carried trade far into the countryside. The livestock economy was dominated by the great fairs of Ballinasloe, Mullingar and Banagher. Ballinasloe and Mullingar were also centres of important wool fairs to which buyers from as far afield as Cork came. In the north, as the linen industry prospered, a large number of markets for linen and yarn emerged in what had formerly been one of the most backward parts of Ireland. In the extreme south butter-buyers paying cash in advance reached even into the more backward districts, and made it possible for tenants to pay cash rents.

Shops in Castle Street, Cork, 1796

As trade grew the ports came to dominate the economy. Not all the ports shared alike in the growth of trade. Business tended to concentrate in the larger ports, and many of the smaller ones suffered. Banking facilities added to the commercial attractions of towns such as Dublin and Cork. As the linen industry rose, the bulk of exports, despite the cost of carriage by cart to Dublin, were handled by merchants in the capital, because access to banking and foreign exchange facilities enabled them to grant credit to the drapers from the north. Indeed, the rise of inland market centres contrasted with the decay of many of the smaller ports. While inland towns were small—Kilkenny alone among them was populous—their economic importance was often out of all proportion to their small size. Retail shops were found only in the towns and larger villages, though the absence of rural shops was in part made good by the presence at fairs and markets of pedlars and itinerant traders. In the Foyle Valley, for instance, there was record in 1748 of 'Hugh Galbraith [who] sells wool hatts and Jas. Vaughan and Robert Forster [who] sells dying stuffs and tobacco in our fairs and marketts'.

The growth of trade resulted in a century of active road-building. Many of the roads built in the busier areas before the 1760s were turnpike roads, financed by capital borrowed on the security of the prospective income from tolls on traffic. But

An Irish road scene, c. 1737

the expenses of building and maintaining such roads were high in relation to the income. From the 1760s the bulk of road-building was financed by a cess or tax levied by the Grand Jury of the county on property-occupiers within the barony concerned. An impressive improvement in roads was evident to contemporaries as the years rolled by. 'For a country so very far behind us as Ireland to have got suddenly so much the start of us in the article of roads, is a spectacle that cannot fail to strike the British traveller exceedingly', declared Young. Twiss, another British traveller of the 1770s, thought the roads 'almost universally as good as those about London'. After the suppression of some marauding bands of outlaws in the early decades of the century, there was no fear of the highwayman on Irish roads, although footpads still lurked in the streets and roads of Dublin and its immediate environs.

The most important single traffic was that in linen from the north to the great Linen Hall in Dublin, the main distributing centre for the home and foreign markets. Striking also was the traffic in wool from Ballinasloe to Cork: in the 1770s, although the trade was already past its peak, '500 cars have been seen in a line'. Larger in bulk was the inland traffic in grain and flour, especially in the second half of the century. A large number of people derived their income from cartage. Many farmers supplemented their income by local carriage. Specialized carters plied between the different centres of trade, carrying any goods on offer, even small parcels. In Strabane, in 1746 'the merchants of this town comonly pay in the winter six shillings per hundred from Dublin to Strabane and in the summer five shillings and sometimes less for goods carried by the carrs'.

Merchants themselves also travelled a good deal to markets and towns. Travel for social purposes also increased disproportionately as movement became easier. Indeed, it was the interest of the gentry in better communications that explained in large measure the liberality with which the grand juries approved cesses for road building. Families no longer lived in semi-isolation but regularly visited neighbouring families as a matter of course for dinners and balls. Young in the 1770s noted that 40 years previously there had been only four carriages in and around Limerick; in the 1770s there were 183 four-wheeled carriages and 115 two-wheeled ones. Many families regularly travelled between their country seats and Dublin, the centre of social life especially during a parliamentary season. Provincial towns were in a more modest way centres of local social life and in season attracted many to them. Mallow, for instance, attracted people of fashion in the summer months to drink the spa waters, and to enjoy its social life, enlivened by frequent race-meetings and an assembly room for dancing, concerts and card-playing. Kilkenny had a gay season with balls and dinners, and its lodging-houses were full.

A sign of easier travel conditions and of the fondness for travel to which they gave birth was the emergence of tourism for the well-to-do. Despite two indifferent inns and uncomfortable lodgings, Killarney was a fashionable place to visit well before the end of the century and was well organized to exploit the tourist with boats and guides for hire. Twiss complained that the two days he spent on the lakes in 1775 cost him eight guineas. To cater for the growing number of travellers, stirred by business or pleasure, Taylor and Skinner's *Maps of the roads of Ireland*

An Irish cart

appeared in 1778, and the *Post-chaise companion; or Traveller's directory through Ireland* in 1784. Stage-coaches running between a number of provincial centres and the capital appeared from the 1750s, such as the 'flying coaches' advertised in 1753 doing the journey between Dublin and Kilkenny in one day. Twiss noted that 'twenty stage-coaches for the conveyance of passengers to various parts of the kingdom had lately been established'. The mails were still carried on horseback by post-boys at this time. In 1757 according to the sub-postmaster at Strabane it was 'generally ten o'clock at night, when my post-boy leaves Strabane, and two in the morning before he arrives at Derry, which when he arrives there, no person will be troubled with him, unless they be overpaid. . . . I allow my rider 14 pounds per year. . . .' The Postmaster-General was exacting in seeing that postmasters and post-boys provided a satisfactory service. The Revenue Commissioners were, for instance, able to keep in touch from Dublin with their offices all over the country with at most a delay of only a few days. In 1747 Stratford Eyre, Governor of Galway, complained of the inconvenience by Galway not having, like other towns in the kingdom, three posts a week. By the end of the century mail-coaches had made their appearance carrying both passengers and mail between the posting stations. In Fermoy, on the main road between Dublin and Cork, horses were provided for six mail-coaches every day.

Despite their relative frequency and the fact that their fares were too high for the ordinary people, the coaches were often full. De Latocnaye, the French traveller, after travelling by stage-coach from Waterford to Gowran to catch the mail-coach from Cork to Dublin found it full and was left behind. Cross-services to supplement the services between provincial towns and Dublin were, however, few (as they are indeed even today in the case of bus and rail services). As a result, travellers often found it necessary to hire a post-chaise. Post-chaises and post-boys were themselves not readily available in all parts: a traveller writing in 1807 noted that 'these accommodations are to be found only on the great roads of communication from one city to another. On the cross-roads he must bear with patience

Turf boat on the Shannon at Limerick

the delays of post-boys, and the indifference of postmasters; his purse will be taxed, and his time lost.' Twiss complained that in 1775 the hire of a post-chaise and horses had cost him four guineas a week, the driver maintaining himself and the horses.

Though the surface of Irish roads was excellent by the standards of the time, enthusiasm often had the better of common sense in planning routes: roads were often laid in a straight line even in hilly country. As a result the gradients were sometimes absurdly precipitate. Young related how, when he was setting out on the road from Knightsbridge to Nedeen, Sir John Coulthurst, whom he had been visiting, sent 'half a dozen labourers with me, to help my chaise up a mountain side, of which he gave a formidable account . . . the labourers, two passing strangers, and my servant could with difficulty get the chaise up.' The comparatively good surface of Irish roads was due more to light industrial traffic than to superior engineering. Not only was there little mineral traffic but goods, instead of being hauled in great four-wheeled wagons by a team of horses as in England, were carried in light two-wheeled carts, each taking 6–12 cwt, hauled by a single horse. A single driver might tend as many as eight horses and carts, the horses feeding along the roadside.

However, some remote areas were still virtually untouched by roads in the eighteenth century. The most important of these areas were the Iveragh Peninsula in co. Kerry, Erris in Mayo, west Donegal and Connemara. Young noted that the barony of Erris was difficult to get into or out of in winter and that few attempted to do so between November and Easter. In areas where roads were non-existent, trade was very limited. Young found that in Carbery, co. Cork, 'provisions are extravagantly cheap from want of communications'. What commercial traffic there was, was carried on horseback or on slide-cars. Butter from Kerry to the Cork market was carried on horseback, with rum and groceries being taken on the return journey. From Muckross the costs were 9*d* a ferkin for butter and 1*s* 8*d* a hundredweight for carriage back from Cork.

Waterways, where available, were everywhere an important means of communication and conveyance. On the estuary of the Shannon in the 1770s 100 boats were active in carrying turf from Kerry and Clare to Limerick. In Connemara much of the commercial traffic was conducted by coastal craft or on the waters of Lough Corrib. Coal from Castlecomer was carried by cart from the collieries to Leighlinbridge and shipped down the Barrow to the tidal port of New Ross. As impediments to navigation were removed, this traffic grew at the expense of the cartage to Dublin by road. Canals were also built. The Newry Canal opened in 1742 from Newry to Lough Neagh never carried the traffic expected, because the coalfield at Coalisland failed to prove a successful venture. The main line of the Grand Canal from Dublin to Shannon was completed in 1804. The Barrow Navigation linking Lowtown on the Grand Canal with Athy on the Barrow had already been completed in 1791. It took some of the coal traffic and also carried flour from the many mills in the Barrow valley.

As early as 1780, when the Grand Canal had only reached Osbertstown, 20 miles from Dublin, the directors of the company decided to set up a passenger service, boats leaving Dublin on Mondays and Thursdays, returning on Tuesdays and Fridays. The first of the canal hotels was opened at Sallins in 1785. Sir John Carr recorded travelling in 1805 from Athy to Dublin on a boat of 'about 35 feet long, having a raised cabin, its roof forming a deck to walk upon . . . we slipped through the water in the most delightful manner imaginable, at the rate of 4 miles an hour.'

Grand Canal Hotel, Portobello

Ploughing and sowing

When the main line was open to Shannon Harbour in 1804, regular services linked Dublin with the Shannon, and hotels were provided at Portobello in Dublin, Robertstown, Tullamore and Shannon Harbour. Thomas Byerley in 1807 related how the boat set out from Dublin at 3 p.m. and reached Robertstown at 9 p.m., where 'I have never seen anything so well conducted, nor any inn so comfortable'. Next morning they set out at 4 o'clock, reaching Shannon Harbour in 12 hours.

For the same reason that the roads were good—relatively light traffic—inns were comparatively few and for the most part indifferent. They were better and more numerous in busy centres such as Kilkenny, but even in Dublin itself visitors at times commented on their poor condition. According to Bush, writing in 1769, 'there is not absolutely one good inn in the town, not one upon my honour, in which an Englishman of any sense of decency would be satisfied with his quarters, and not above two or three in the whole city that he could bear to be in'. People staying for a period generally took lodgings. The Earl of Abercorn was advised in March 1746 that it would not be 'easy to gett such lodgings as you may be pleas'd with especially as they must be furnished with table linnen which is as I am informed seldom expected, and will much enhance the price ... they are vastly extravagant in the time of Parliament, but they abate as the sessions draw to a conclusion.' Young declared 'good lodgings almost as dear as they are in London; though we were well accommodated (dirt excepted) for two guineas and an half a week. All the lower ranks in this city have no idea of English cleanliness, either in apartments, persons or cookery.'

Despite the growth of trade, agriculture was a highly conservative business and archaic methods died slowly. Burning straw to shed the grain and ploughing by the tail, although disappearing, were not unknown in the eighteenth century. Yet some of the deficiencies of Irish farming were not so much the result of bad management as of a want of capital. Small farmers relied too heavily on repeated croppings of corn that exhausted the soil, because they had not sufficient capital to build up a herd of animals to diversify their farming. Inadequate manuring of the land was not due simply to ignorance of the merits of manuring but to the fact that, as farm buildings were few and animals left in the open, little manure was collected. Farmers were very active in liming land, or in areas where soil was wet or sticky, mixing limestone gravel into it. Some enlightened landlords were at considerable expense in encouraging tenants to use lime. At Collon in co. Louth, Sir John Foster had 27 kilns burning lime for his tenants, and paid £700 a year for fuel for the kilns. But with or without encouragement from their landlords many farmers spent much time in carting lime and in spreading it on their land.

Moreover, farmers were able to make do with little equipment. Hard work, often combined with a little ingenuity, made up for the defects in what they had. An estate agent in Strabane in 1764 described how a small tenant who had a field in a bog 'is now drawing gravel on it, which before, chiefly on account of his poverty, and partly its not being able to bear a horse, he carried on his back'. In mountain areas it was impossible to use a plough, and in the south-west ten men using a *loy* or spade could dig up an acre in a day. Even the defective ploughs were, with ingenuity and attention, made to do their work. At Castlemartyr, according to Young, 'they plough generally with four horses, sow with two, and use ploughs of so bad a construction that a man attends them with a strong stick leaning on the beam to keep it in the ground'. Despite his criticisms of Irish agriculture, Young had to admit that the Irish farmers 'are uncommon masters of the art of overcoming difficulties by patience and contrivance . . . give the farmer of 20 acres in England no more capital than his brother in Ireland, and I will

Haymaking

venture to say he will be much poorer, for he would be utterly unable to go on at all'.

Within rural areas agriculture was far from being the sole occupation of all the inhabitants. Smiths, carpenters, nail-makers, thatchers, masons, were numerous. The smith in particular, making or repairing a variety of agricultural or household goods, was of especial importance. The most widespread manufacturing activity was in the textile industry. In remote areas families spun and wove in order to clothe themselves. In other areas families spun or wove for the market. In the south of Ireland weaving for the market was largely confined to Dublin, Carrick and a number of areas in co. Cork. But combing and spinning wool into yarn for the English market was widespread. The wool was put out by merchants, and women, spinning in their houses, could make up to 2d or 3d a day. This, low though the remuneration was, was a valuable supplement to incomes in many parts of Ireland, and where such employment did not exist for women and children, rural families were worse off.

In the north of the country the growth of the linen industry was responsible for a widespread diffusion of weaving skills in rural parts in the eighteenth century. The linen industry was almost entirely domestic except for the finishing or bleaching of the cloth, which required expensive machinery and was in the hands of well-to-do bleachers. The bulk of the weaving was done in the counties of the north-east; in the remaining counties of the north the weaving was less well organized and the cloth inferior. The demand for yarn encouraged a rapid development of spinning reaching out of Ulster into Connaught and north Leinster. Spinning was done by women and children, and in eastern Donegal and in Fermanagh also many of the farmers kept farm-servants at wages of up to £3 per annum to do the housework and to spin yarn from the flax. If the price of yarn was unduly low, the farmers often wove it into cloth themselves. The main centres were, however, the counties of Down and Armagh, and they depended on an inflow of yarn from west Ulster and from Connaught. Young deplored the combination of weaving and farming by, as he put it, weavers 'who cultivate, or rather beggar the soil, as well as work the looms'. But with rising population and small farms farmers could not have fared well from farming alone in the comparatively densely populated counties of eastern Ulster.

The weavers sold the cloth unbleached on the numerous linen markets which sprang up in the north-east as the trade expanded. The markets were attended by drapers, who bought the cloth and commissioned a bleacher to finish it. Young provided a vivid picture of how business was transacted at the market in Lurgan where 'when the clock strikes eleven the drapers jump upon stone standings, and the weavers instantly flock about them with their pieces'.

There was much poverty in Ireland in the first 40 years of the century. Agricultural prices generally were low. If farmers did not fare even worse, it was only because some of them reduced the amount of tillage in favour of pasturage, as cattle prices were more buoyant than grain prices. Many contemporaries were, however, alarmed by the decline in tillage. The 1720s were a decade of recurrent scarcity and 1728–29 itself was a year of famine. At the time all this was blamed on a decline in tillage.

Hillmount bleachgreen and house

Brown linen market at Banbridge

In fact, the high prices and famine conditions had been caused by a general harvest failure in these islands, and not by a reduction of tillage which alarmist opinion greatly exaggerated. In many years Irish farmers were embarrassed by an over-bountiful harvest. The decline in tillage never went as far as some contemporaries suggested. Much of the increase in cattle numbers was at the expense of sheep-farming, made unattractive by the rise in sheep numbers in England. Many farmers, moreover, did not have the capital to buy livestock, and especially in areas with urban markets to hand farmers were slow to reduce tillage. Grain was important in the Irish diet in mid-century; the potato, though important, especially for the poor, was subsidiary.

The extensive famine of 1740–41 was a consequence of failure of the harvest. Suffering was very severe. In Dublin the weekly number of burials, normally below 50, ran as high as 200. News of death from famine or fever came in from most parts of the country. By March 1741 it was reported from Loughrea that 'many through want perish daily in the roads and ditches, where they are buried'. From Dunloe on the Kenmare estate in April 1741 the complaint came that 'there is not a tenant on Lower Lakard able to pay 20*s*, most of them being dead'. In 1744 the harvest failed disastrously again. By April 1745 it was reported from Strabane that 'the poor are in great distress, many eating the flesh of dead carrion cattle', and the price of oatmeal had risen from 4*d* a peck to 20*d*. Yet though many suffered hardship and high prices affected all, few died of hunger in 1745, because the harvest in England had not failed and imports of grain and meal soared in the first half of 1745 to what was to be their highest level for the eighteenth century.

The physical appearance of the countryside altered in the course of the century. After mid-century especially there was much enclosure, the remaining large open tracts of land being divided into neat fields by ditches topped with quicksets or by stone walls. Even the great sheep-walks, reduced to some extent by the encroachment of arable farming, were already partially enclosed: according to Young 'the country [i.e. co. Roscommon] is divided into inclosures by stone walls generally, so that one shepherd is all that is kept to a flock'. One reason for the changing appearance of the country was the accelerated rise of population from mid-century, leading to a more intensified use of land. Greater population also meant more housebuilding, thus adding to the changes afoot in rural Ireland. Landlords often took an intelligent interest in their estates. Many of them eliminated middlemen, and the estates of many absentees, especially the estates of peers, were well managed by professional estate agents. Landlords, both resident and absentee, took an interest in the development of industry, seeking to establish industries on their estates, spending money both on the building of cottages for workers and in attracting skilled workmen. The model estate villages, sometimes with an elegant market-house, testify further to the improving spirit of the age, and many of the villages and small towns outside the main areas of trade were either creations of landlords or owed much to their encouragement.

The towns in an age of expanding trade changed no less than the countryside. New streets, new houses and new public buildings were being laid out in most towns. Of Dundalk, Young remarked that 'the place, like most of the Irish towns I have been in, [is] full of new buildings'. The results of urban expansion were that the old walls, already decaying, were quickly pulled down, and their stones used as building material. Moreover, some of the

Fire-fighting in the eighteenth century

towns were entirely new, their rise being due to expanding markets or fairs or to the benevolence and interest of a local landlord. Formerly, some of these towns had consisted of a mere hamlet of a few indifferent cabins. In Killarney, before the Earl of Kenmare improved it, 'there were not six slate houses in the village, but mostly mud cabins, low and ill-thatched'. Galway and Limerick were exceptional among the older towns in the first half of the century because, as the surrounding districts were held to be disaffected, the walls were still kept in a state of repair, the gates closed at night and sentinels posted. The fact that Ireland remained peaceful during the Jacobite invasion of England in 1745 proved, however, that these fears had been groundless and the walls soon lost their military importance. In Limerick, which was an expanding town, this led quickly to the pulling down of the walls, and a well-laid-out new town began to take shape alongside the old town with its narrow streets. In Galway, expanding more slowly, the walls came down less rapidly. Coquebert de Montbret, visiting the town in 1791, noted that 'a great rampart with bastions still stands around the town'. But the walls already presented a picture of decay. The only town which retained its walls in a good state of repair was

Derry, where 'the ancient ramparts are not demolished but form at present an agreeable walk'. De Latocnaye, to whom we owe this comment, thought that the town could be made more healthy by levelling them and 'affording a supply of fresh air', but he noted that 'the inhabitants consider them as a glorious monument which reminds them of the siege this city held against King James'.

With few exceptions the ports were the largest and busiest of the towns. Inland towns were often busy market centres, but their resident population was small, and they had little industry. While the textile industries were all inland, their organization was domestic, and the main function the towns had was as market centres, where cloth or yarn was gathered together before final disposal in the markets of the port towns. Coal-mining was conducted on a small scale at a few centres, only at Castlecomer with any conspicuous degree of success. Ironworks burning charcoal had been fairly numerous, but they declined rapidly as the woodlands were used up, and for want of charcoal the surviving works were unable to operate continuously. Otherwise, the only widely dispersed industries were the processing of agricultural raw materials such as soap-

The walls of Derry

boiling, candle-making, grain-milling, and distilling. The last two industries expanded rapidly in the second half of the century. Many

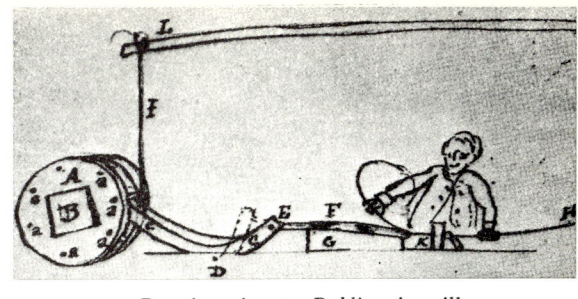

Drawing wire at a Dublin wire-mill

flour-mills, large and small, were erected. With a growing substitution of Irish whiskey for imported spirits, a highly commercialized whiskey industry was also making its appearance: at Kilcock, for instance, Young saw 'six great distilleries for making whiskey'.

Not all the ports shared alike in the expansion of trade. There was a pronounced tendency for the larger ports to gain at the expense of the smaller. So important was their role that until the closing decades of the century the bulk of linen exports from the north passed through the Dublin market, and only in the early nineteenth century did the trade in the north free itself from financial dependence on Dublin. The port towns were active centres of industries using imported raw materials: sugar-refining, brewing, glass-blowing, salt-refining and iron-founding. As early as the 1750s Dublin had 12 paper-mills; in the 1770s it had five foundries and in the 1790s about a dozen sugar-refineries. Other ports had similar activity, although on a smaller scale. Cork, the second port in the island, was noted more for its trade than for its industry, however. Some 700 coopers were employed making barrels into which to pack the salt beef, pork and butter exported from the port. Young found Cork 'the busiest, most animated scene of shipping in all Ireland'. De Latocnaye thought it 'a very gloomy and dirty city', and added that 'you are every moment stopped by funerals, droves of cattle, or beggars, who go through the streets by dozens, and yet this city is one of the richest and most commercial in Europe'.

Dublin easily outstripped any other town in size or wealth. Its population had almost doubled to 130,000 by 1750, and was around 200,000 at the end of the century: house-building was very active in the capital throughout the century. It was

View of B. Sullivan's paper manufactory, ironworks, and foundry, Beechmount, near Cork

already an impressive city in the early decades. An English socialite lady who came to live in Dublin in the early 1730s thought St Stephen's Green 'may be preferred justly to any in London; it is a great deal larger than Lincoln's Inn Fields', and considered the Phoenix Park 'far beyond St James or Hyde Park'. Its new public buildings such as the Parliament House, the Exchange and the façade of Trinity College impressed visitors, and as a result of the efforts of the Wide Streets Commissioners, appointed in 1757, some of its streets were very fine. Young stated that 'the public buildings are magnificent, very many of the streets regularly laid out, and exceedingly well built'. But at this time the prevailing picture was still one of narrow cramped streets, dirty and disagreeable, ill-lit and dangerous at night. Luckombe stated that 'except the few new streets, which are paved and flagged like those of London, the whole of it is abominably dirty and slippery'. According to Young himself, some of whose com-

Cutting and packing meat for export, Cork

ments on the city had been so favourable, 'walking in the streets there, from the narrowness and populousness of the principal thoroughfares, as well as from the dirt and wretchedness of the *canaille*, is a most uneasy and disgusting exercise'.

Yet it must be noted that, when Young visited Dublin, the most impressive works of the Wide Streets Commissioners had not yet been undertaken, and the Paving Board, appointed in 1773 'for paving, cleaning, lighting, draining, and improving the streets', had only begun its work. Moreover, a whole new city was taking shape to the east of the old axis stretching from the Castle to the south and Capel Street to the north. Ground landlords insisted in the leases they granted on conformity in new buildings with certain requirements, thus ensuring in the absence of any municipal regulation a remarkable harmony. On the north side new squares and thoroughfares were taking shape on the Gardiner estate. The Mall (now Upper O'Connell Street) was built originally as an elongated residential square, but by its extension to the Liffey by the laying out of Lower Sackville Street in 1784 and by the approaches to the north to the new square called Rutland Square between 1784 and 1790 a magnificent new thoroughfare was created. When this was linked by the Carlisle Bridge in 1791 to the new streets already laid out on the south side by the Commissioners (D'Olier Street and Westmoreland Street), a new main north–south axis had been created, and traffic flowed along wide streets between Rutland Square on the north and the new residential areas already established around the Green and on the Molesworth

Westmoreland Street and D'Olier Street seen from Carlisle Bridge

estate in the first half of the century and new ones growing on the Fitzwilliam estate.

Three main districts were now beginning to emerge in Dublin, an elegant and spacious residential area on the north side, another on the far side of the Liffey to the south-east, and thirdly on the far side of the Liffey to the south-west, in the old city and its 'liberties', a mass of narrow streets and crowded tenements. In the last district the houses in the lanes and alleys leading off the streets were inhabited by working 'manufacturers, by petty shopkeepers, the labouring poor, and beggars crowded together to a degree distressing to humanity'. As early as 1729 Dobbs had noted that '70 persons have been known to live in a house, there being a family sometimes in each room, often times in each floor, and in the cellars'. The sanitary condition of these parts of the city showed little improvement at the end of the century: 'into the backyard of each house, frequently not 10 feet deep, is flung from the windows of each apartment, the ordure and other filth of its numerous inhabitants; from which it is so seldom removed, that I have seen it nearly on a level with the windows of the first floor.' The contrast between the new and the decaying

High Street, Belfast, 1786

districts was not confined to Dublin. De Latocnaye had thought that 'the new town of Limerick is very pretty and regular, but the old one is equally ugly and dirty'.

Despite the presence of much poverty, an air of confidence and a belief in continued improvement was evident in the late eighteenth century. Some of this feeling was of course naïve. The English visitor, Bush, for instance, had commented 'on the ridiculous vanity of pretending to speak better English' than in London. Gamble in 1810 had noted that 'vanity seems the prominent feature of every inhabitant of Dublin; he is vain of

BUYE the dry Turf; buye Turf; buye the dry Turf—Here's the dry Bog-a-Wood.—Here's the Chips to light the Fire; Maids!

Turf sales in Dublin

himself, vain of his city, of its beauty, of the splendour of its public buildings, of its vast superiority over London in this respect.' A Dubliner of the late eighteenth century would have found it difficult to conceive that the following century should be one of sharp relative decline for his city. Yet so it proved to be. The Union of 1800, resulting in the extinction of the Dublin Parliament, was not reflected in any immediate ill-effects, and decline, as it became evident, was in fact due to a whole complex of factors.

Further Reading

S. Andrews, *Nine generations, a history of the Andrews family, millers of Comber*, 1958

M. Craig, *Dublin, 1660–1860, a social and architectural history*, 1952

—— *The personality of Leinster*, 1961

TOWN AND COUNTRY IN THE EIGHTEENTH CENTURY

L. M. Cullen, *An economic history of Ireland since 1660*, 1972

L. M. Cullen, 'Problems in the interpretation and revision of eighteenth-century Irish economic history', in *Transactions of the Royal Historical Society*, 5th series, vol. XVII, 1967

M. Drake, 'Marriage and population growth in Ireland, 1750–1845', in *Economic History Review*, 2nd series, vol. XVI, no. ii, 1963

C. Gill, *Rise of the Irish linen industry*, 1925

E. R. R. Green, *Industrial archaeology of county Down*, 1963

Lansdowne, Marquis of, *Glanerought and the Petty-Fitzmaurices*, 1937

C. Maxwell, *Dublin under the Georges, 1714–1830*, 1937

―― *Town and country in Ireland under the Georges*, 1949

D. F. Moore, *Dublin*, 1965

G. Murphy, 'The Gaelic background', in M. Tierney (ed.), *D. O'Connell: nine centenary essays*, 1949

A. Young, *Tour in Ireland* (2 vols, ed. A. W. Hutton, 1892)

V

Life in the Eighteenth Century

Land and its ownership were of central importance in the economy and society. Even the nobility and the well-to-do gentry with town-houses spent much of their time on their estates. Industry was to a large extent carried on in the countryside. The expanding linen industry was a rural one, and its success contrasted with the woollen industry which in its most commercialized branches was town-based. In 1725 the eight largest towns contained only 30,246 houses out of a total of 386,229 in the island. Not only was wealth associated with land, but landownership determined political power. Landed families dominated the county constituencies and the boroughs with their even more restricted franchise. While the electorate was small, constituencies were sometimes fiercely contested by rival family interests. The greater of the Irish peers were at the head of small groups of sons, brothers or relatives elected to the House of Commons.

One of the prime features of the Irish scene was the upheaval in landownership which took place in the seventeenth century. As a result of the confiscation of lands owned by Irish and 'old English' families, only one-seventh of the land was in Catholic hands by 1702, and misfortune had thus helped to obliterate the already vanishing differences between the old Irish families and later arrivals who had in part dispossessed them. The difficulties of the surviving Catholic proprietors were considerable. By law they could not buy land; at the death of the father lands were divided equally between all the sons, and if the eldest son turned Protestant, his father became a mere tenant for life. Evasion of the laws was, despite 'discoveries', possible. But as the fourth Viscount Kenmare wrote in 1755, 'I ever avoided meddling in purchases as I scarce know the trustee I would depend on and wrangles of roguery on this head might stagger a man in the most determined resolution of (what is of all matters the most essential) his religion.' It is hardly surprising in such circumstances that many Catholic proprietors changed their religion to preserve their lands or their political influence.

Handicaps to business enterprise by Catholics, though they existed, were not as serious, and in the ports especially Catholics were frequently among the merchants who prospered. Laws regarding property did not greatly affect the mass of the ordinary people. It is true of course that, for the greater part of the century, Catholics could not take land on a lease exceeding 31 years. But this affected mainly well-to-do Catholics, who aspired to make a profit by reletting land more than it affected the occupying tenants for whom a lease for 31 years was advantageous, and who, when prices were rising, stood to gain considerably in the interval before renewal. For the ordinary people the most tangible disability was that they were by law

Group of eighteenth-century gentlemen

Catholic chapel at Ardglass, co. Carlow, 1794

compelled to pay tithes to the clergy of the Church of Ireland. This disability, however, Catholics shared with the Dissenters in the north.

In theory comprehensive legislation existed restricting Catholic worship in the eighteenth century. A single registered clergyman was permitted in a parish, unregistered clergymen and all ecclesiastical dignitaries were banished, and education for the priesthood or the return of clergy from the Continent was proscribed. But in practice persecution broke down, and even unregistered clergymen were able to carry out their functions. Attempts at enforcement of these laws enjoyed little consistent support from the authorities themselves, and ran into vigorous opposition from Catholics. Of a priest-hunter in Dublin in 1711 we read that 'the aforesaid rioters or popish mob pursued the said Oxenard thro' several streets of this city, crying out "priest-catcher", and thereupon threw stones, brick batts and dirt at him'.

In such circumstances it is scarcely surprising that the number of clergy rose, and that Catholic chapels increased in number as well. In 1731 40 Mass houses were reported in the Archdiocese of Cashel, 'several of them very lately built, some new buildings, particularly one at Tipperary in the form of a cross 92 feet by 72'. In Tuam there were 'mass houses in most parishes, in some more than one'. In the Archdiocese of Dublin, there were, apart from chapels in the city and its 'liberties', 58 Mass houses, of which 24 had been built since 1714. The chapels were unpretentious buildings, in the towns generally in the back streets. Mass in many places, as in much of the Diocese of Derry in 1731, was read 'in the open fields or under some shed set up occasionally for shelter'. This was not caused, however, by the need to evade the authorities. It was a consequence either of poverty or of the difficulty, if landowners proved bigoted, of acquiring a site for a chapel. Orders for the closing of the chapels were issued only in the short-lived periods of political tension when a Jacobite descent on these islands was feared. By 1745 even this urge had spent itself. During the Jacobite invasion of Britain in that year, no order was issued by the authorities for the closing of the chapels. Active persecution was over, and, with a time-lag of about a generation, this was slowly reflected in a removal of most of the civil and some of the political disabilities of Catholics. In 1778 Catholics were allowed to hold long leases; in 1782 to purchase land. In 1793 the professions were opened and Catholics acquired the right to vote, although not the right to be elected to Parliament.

In no respect was the failure of the penal restrictions more evident than in education. By law schoolmastering by Catholics, the maintenance of a tutor by Catholic families or the sending of Catholics overseas for education were all prohibited. But in practice better-off Catholics had no difficulty in going to France or Spain for their education, nor did they run into any danger in returning. There were also ample opportunities of having an elementary education from Catholic schoolmasters at home. The only openings for educated Catholics were, however, the priesthood itself, commissions in the French or other European armies, or the medical profession after study at one of the European universities. Catholics were excluded from Trinity College, and of Catholics educated abroad only physicians could hope to practise in Ireland. The demand for an education suitable for these openings was especially marked in the southwest, where in the dairying districts relatively large numbers of Catholics were able to take advantage of letting dairy cattle to dairymen to acquire a modest competence, which enabled them to think in more ambitious terms for the education of their children. A great Catholic landowner in co. Kerry himself spoke scornfully of 'the pride, drunkenness and sloth of the middling sort among the Irish. Every one of them thinks himself too great for any industry except taking farms. When they happen to get them they screw enormous rents from some beggarly dairyman and spend their whole time in the alehouse of the next village. If they have sons they are all to be priests, physicians or French officers.'

Schoolmasters were numerous. Donnchadh Ruadh Mac Conmara, a poet-schoolmaster of co. Waterford in the second half of the century, in parodying the names of other schoolmasters in his neighbourhood, suggests how numerous they were in a single district: Christopher Mac Heavy-bottom, Giddyhead O'Hackett, Coxcomb O'Boland, Tatter O'Flanagan, Dirty, puffy John O'Mulrooney, Blear-eyed O'Cullenan and Giggler O'Mulcahy. Landlords or their agents did not always welcome popular education. An agent in the south-west complained to his landlord: 'as to school masters, we have too many, and too many mere scholars, for we abound with schools and schoolboys, and it would be better that our youth should be hammering at the anvil than at bog latin.' While landlord or agent on occasion resented schooling because it interfered with the supply of amenable labour for the rude tasks of the countryside, it should be recognized that in fact the rural environment offered little scope for the man of some education and no means. Schoolmastering itself attracted many who were literate, but who could hope to find no other outlet for their talents and no prospects of betterment.

The absence of opportunity was only in part due to the operation of the Penal Laws which deprived Catholics of employment under municipal or State auspices, including even menial posts in the Revenue establishment. The fundamental cause was economic: outlets in clerical employment were extremely limited in a predominantly rural society and for the educated Catholic without the resources to aspire to an army commission or a career abroad, prospects were narrow in the extreme. In such circumstances the only outlet was the priesthood or, if that did not appeal, schoolmastering. The poet Sean

The country schoolmaster

O'Coileáin (1754–1817) had, for instance, been sent to Spain to study for the priesthood, and not proceeding with this intention became, in his early twenties, a schoolmaster at Myross between Castlehaven and Glandore in co. Cork. Few were able to obtain clerical employment. Seán na Raithíneach O'Murchadha was employed as a clerk and later as a bailiff in co. Cork until he threw the post up: 'since I am a poet, down through the lack of the nobles, I will run to my garden, take spade in hand, and to the devil with bailiffing'. Donnchadh Ruadh Mac Conmara, another poet, who in his youth had been sent to Rome to study for the priesthood, for a time renounced his faith in order to obtain the parish clerkship in the Protestant church at Rossmire.

For the establishment of a school the capital required was negligible. The schoolmaster either rented or built a hut which served the purpose of school-house, or in better organized areas one was provided by the parish. De Latocnaye, a French traveller in the 1790s, noted that the school-house was 'generally a poor hut without a window', and that for this reason on fine days teacher and scholars chose to apply themselves in the open air. Young had written 20 years earlier that he had seen 'many a ditch full of scholars'. A school-house was built at Cross Roads, co. Kilkenny, for Dennis O'Sullivan, a schoolmaster lately arrived from Kerry in the summer of 1791. 'In truth', says his schoolmaster-shopkeeper son, Humphrey, 'it was a small school house, some 20 feet by ten. The sod walls were put up on the first day, the timber roofing on the second, and the thatch on the third. And many a long uneventful day my father spent teaching in this hovel, in another mud-walled cabin somewhat larger at the Tree of Killaloe, and in a good schoolhouse in Ballykeefe.'

According to Young, schools were 'everywhere to be met

with, where reading and writing are taught'. A letter in poetic form sent by Eoghan Ruadh O'Súilleabháin to Fr Ned Fitzgerald, asking him to publish from the altar that he was about to open a school at Knocknagree in co. Kerry, furnishes an idea of the teaching:

> *Reverend Sir –*
> *Please to publish from the altar of your holy Mass*
> *that I will open school at Knocknagree Cross,*
> *Where the tender babes will be well off,*
> *For it's there I'll teach them their criss-cross;*
> *Reverend Sir, you will by experience find*
> *All my endeavours to please mankind.*
> *For it's there I will teach them how to read and write.*

Eoghan offered still more:

> *To forward them with speed and care,*
> *With book-keeping and mensuration,*
> *Euclid's Elements and navigation,*
> *With trigonometry and sound gauging.*

And last of all:

> *And sweet love letters for the ladies.*

Some schools were seminaries for the priesthood. 'Schools are also common for men', noted Young. 'I have seen a dozen great fellows at school, and was told that they were educating with an intention of being priests.' This explains also the emphasis on Latin and Greek in some of the elementary schools, especially in the south-west. In Galway in 1791 Coquebert de Montbret noted that 'each chapel has a schoolmaster who teaches the Catechism in Irish, but there are not good classical schools as they are in Kerry, or even Mayo.'

Some contemporaries were greatly impressed by the growth of schools. Richard Lovell Edgeworth, for instance, noting at the end of the eighteenth century 'prodigious improvement' in Ireland, declared that 20 persons could read or write for one 20 years previously. This is too optimistic an assessment. Nevertheless, the 1841 Census shows that of the survivors of the age group who were between 5 and 15 years between 1781 and 1790, 52 per cent of the males, and 31 per cent of the females, could read or write. As early as 1821, judging by the Census of that year, almost one-quarter of the age group between those years attended school. Many of course attended school only intermittently, or for a short period. This meant that the number who received some schooling was much larger than might be inferred from attendances recorded at the decennial National Census. In the more prosperous east of Ireland this was reflected in more widespread literacy. In the poorer regions, however, intermittent attendance seriously affected the quality of the education. Although school attendance as early as 1821 was as high in Kerry and Cork as in more prosperous counties, literacy, as the 1841 census data suggest, was much lower. In such regions, in some measure in consequence of these conditions, schoolmastering was an unremunerative profession, the masters themselves restless or disposed to move further afield or intermittently to give up teaching altogether. In the case of Eoghan Ruadh O'Súilleabháin, teaching was combined with intermittent bouts of activity as a migrant labourer.

Few of these humble schoolmasters progressed as did Brian Merriman from farming and school-teaching in co. Clare into cities like Limerick, where as a teacher of mathematics his death in 1805 was considered notable enough to be recorded in a newspaper. Nevertheless, if often of poor quality or intermittent, education had become widespread by the late eighteenth century. In many districts its provision had ceased to be haphazard, and was organized under parish auspices or from the early nineteenth century entrusted to Orders of brothers or nuns, who were now beginning to make their appearance in Irish popular education. The rapid expansion of education from the 1840s, as measured in the figures of the Board of National Education, is explicable in terms of a broad and not altogether ineffective base already established.

Not all the education available was provided by popular schools. The so-called 'Charter' schools, which received their Royal Charter in 1733 and enjoyed financial assistance from the Irish Parliament, were working with the object that 'the children of the popish and other poor natives . . . may be instructed in the English language and in the principles of true religion and loyalty in all succeeding generations'. In addition to imparting an education on such principles they were also to train children 'in labour and

Turnip, a celebrated gelding

industry in order to cure that habitual laziness and idleness which is too common among the poor in this country'. There were in all some 50 of these schools. But because of their proselytizing policy they attracted few Catholic inmates. Moreover, their management was inefficient and negligent, and neither Protestant nor Catholic pupil can have fared well. In the 1780s the children were reported to be 'generally ill-fed, ill-clad and ill-taught, sickly, pale, miserable objects, a disgrace to all society'. Some landlords or their wives took an interest in education, and even maintained schools. In the towns, especially Dublin, there were also private schools for the well-to-do.

Social life in town no less than in country revolved round the landed classes. In Dublin, this was in striking evidence during the parliamentary sessions, which attracted to the capital not only the peers and members of the Commons, but others who wished to attach themselves to the gay life of the season. Absenteeism was far less common among the landed proprietors than was often assumed to be the case.

Boisterous living, far from being taken for granted, was coming to be an object of censure as the century passed. Many visitors commented on excessive drinking being less prevalent than they had been led to believe. As for gambling, much of it took place at the race-meetings which were very popular with the gentry and had a large popular following as well. Of co. Derry in 1750 we read that 'there was lately a very great cock match and racing at Derry where this town and country lost considerably amongst whom I am assured John Hamilton Esquire of Munterlong lost above £400'. The middlemen, living on profit-rents from the reletting of land, were the worst element in Irish rural society. Young spoke of them as 'your fellows with round hats, edged with gold, who hunt in the morning, get drunk in the evening and fight the next morning'. These were 'the masters of packs of wretched hounds, and it is a notorious fact, that they are the hardest drinkers in Ireland'. But their number and influence were declining in the late eighteenth century. Moreover, they had never been really numerous except in the south-west, where, by letting herds of cattle to impoverished dairymen, they had played an important role in the expansion of the dairy industry.

The 'gambling, wine drinking, pipe, viol, and harp music' mentioned in Carolan's song in praise of Hewlett must have represented for many the norm of social life in the early eighteenth century. Houses, though larger and roomier than in the past, were still utilitarian and cheerless. Mrs Pendarves (the future Mrs Delany) noted that the 'people of this country don't seem solicitous of having good dwellings or more furniture than is absolutely necessary'. Farm buildings often surrounded the dwelling and even as late as the end of the 1770s Young commented on many cases of 'the residence surrounded by walls, or hedges, or cabbins'. But change was taking place nevertheless. The building of large, spacious and elegant country-houses began as early as the 1720s, and did not lose pace. Young commented that 'the number of new ones just built, or building, is prodigiously great'. Terracing and gardening also came into vogue, and Scottish gardeners were especially prized for their skill. Interiors no less than exteriors aspired to be elegant. Walls and ceilings were decorated with plasterwork, skilled furniture-makers catered for the demand for lighter and more agreeable furniture, and the houses of the well-to-do were filled, sometimes discriminatingly, sometimes less so, with Italian sculpture and painting.

Reading had become common. The newspapers catered for a limited but, within the landed classes, widespread demand for information. Pamphlets and books had a growing audience, and many of the more cultivated gentry were able to make their own contributions to the pamphlet literature which was at the

Members of the family of Richard Lovell Edgeworth, including his daughter, Maria

centre of eighteenth-century controversy on political and economic issues. Literacy reached to the womenfolk of the landed classes no less than to the men. Of the widow of Speaker Conolly of Castletown House who died in 1752, Mrs Delany wrote: 'we have just lost our great Mrs Conolly . . . she was clever at business, wrote all her own letters, and read a newspaper by candlelight without spectacles.' The fact that spectacles were coming into use is itself a comment on the times. An agent in a comparatively remote town in co. Donegal, Lifford, wrote in 1758 to his landlord in London: 'I return your Lordship my humblest thanks for the spectacles you were so good as to send me, which I beleive will be of great service; ther was no good ones to be gott in this country.'

Against this background a serious interest in estate management was common. For some it was a hobby no less than a business preoccupation. The Orrerys of Caledon, co. Tyrone, were said to be 'both fond of the country; she delights in farming, and he in building and gardening, and he has very good taste.' Sir James Caldwell related in 1772 how he went 'to dine with Lord Clanbrassill, and met him in the fields up to his knees in wet and dirt, with hatchet under his arm, having been all day pruning trees'. A practical interest in estate management and in wider agricultural improvement was responsible for the establishment of the Dublin Society in 1731. Many of the gentry supervised the building of their own homes. Gandon, the English architect who came to Dublin in the second half of the century and who designed some of the city's finest buildings, declared that 'the gentry are almost always their own architects'.

Hospitality was still lavish. Mrs Clayton, wife of the Bishop of Killala, in her house on St Stephen's Green, kept 'a very handsome table, six dishes of meat at dinner, and six plates at supper'. But the emphasis was moving to refinement. At Carton, home of the Duke of Leinster, French horns played during dinner. Tea and coffee had made their appearance and helped in the softening of domestic manners. Their success in this direction was, however, partial, as much time was still spent by the gentlemen over the table with their claret after dinner. 'If a gentleman likes tea or coffee', according to Young, 'he retires without saying any thing.'

The performance of plays within the circle of family and friends was not uncommon. Balls, to which neighbouring families came, helped to enliven the social life of rural areas, and some of the provincial towns developed a strong social life with a season of theatre, balls and assemblies, attracting landed families from the monotony of a wide hinterland. The peak of Irish social life was the Dublin season, especially during a parliamentary session. In the season of 1782 'nothing can be so gay as Dublin is—the Castle twice a week, the opera twice a week, with plays, assemblies and suppers to fill up the time'. Life was much more informal and free than in London. Mrs Pendarves thought that 'there is a heartiness among them that is more like Cornwall than any I have known'. A feature often commented on by visitors was overcrowding at social events. Young found that 'you almost everywhere meet a company much too numerous for the size of the apartments'. De Latocnaye, a French visitor, spoke of assemblies 'where from the street-door to the garret every room was full of handsome well-dressed ladies, so closely stowed that they could hardly

Harp Festival in the Assembly Room, Belfast, 10-13 July 1792

stir and spoke through their fans'. These conditions even applied to the entertainments given by the Lord-Lieutenant in the Castle. In 1732 at supper-time at a ball 'when the doors were first opened the hurly-burly is not to be described; sqawking, shrieking, all sorts of noises; some ladies lost their lappets, others were trod upon'.

A fondness for music was general. The interest among the upper classes in harp music represented a link of continuity with the pattern of culture and entertainment which was fast dying in the early decades of the century. Carolan (1670–1738), the blind harper who accompanied his own compositions, was received in the homes of Gaelic and Anglo-Irish families alike. The Delanys, for instance, kept an Irish harper in the house of their deanery in the Diocese of Down, who played to them at meal-times or to Mrs Delany while she was drawing. Dr Delany was also a patron of Carolan, and after the harper's death was responsible for bringing out an edition of his music. Prominent society people themselves performed music in the

Pony-races at the Theatre Royal, Crowe Street

Charitable Music Society which met in the Bull's Tavern in Fishamble Street, and it was at the Society's new Music Hall in that street that in 1742 Handel's *Messiah* was first publicly performed 'for the relief of the prisoners in the several gaols and for the support of Mercer's Hospital . . . and of the Charitable Infirmary'. For the occasion the hall was packed with some 700 people. Enthusiasm was not, however, confined to such a momentous occasion. In St Patrick's Cathedral on St Cecilia's Day in 1731 for a performance of the *Te Deum* and *Jubilate* of Purcell and the concertos of Corelli, Mrs Pendarves noted that 'we were there in the greatest crowd I ever saw . . . we went at 10 and stayed till 4'.

Commonplace and universal though poverty was, there were many in town and country outside the ranks of the well-to-do, whose resources, though slender, were sufficient to prevent them from living in dire straits. The houses of the ordinary people in rural areas were far from all falling into the category of wretched mud-cabins without chimney or windows. Two-storey houses or stone dwellings with slated roofs were not uncommon in the eastern half of the country. Mud walls themselves were not uncomfortable. With walls 18 inches to two feet thick, such houses, according to Young, 'when they are well roofed, and

LIFE IN THE EIGHTEENTH CENTURY

built not of stones, ill put together, but of mud . . . are much warmer, independently of smoak, than the clay or lath and mortar cottages of England'. Chimneys were now beginning to become common, although in the poorer western regions or in other areas among the destitute or very poor who built on the roadside, houses with no outlet for the smoke except through a hole in the roof or through the door were still common. Nor were the animals invariably lodged indoors with the inhabitants at night. According to Young 'the luxury of sties is coming in in Ireland, which excludes the poor pigs from the warmth of the bodies of their master and mistress: I remarked little hovels of earth thrown up near the cabbins.' In south Wexford especially 'the cabbins were generally much better than any I had seen in Ireland: large ones with two or three rooms, in good order and repair, all with windows and chimnies and little styes, for their pigs or cattle.'

Among the small farmers, as opposed to cottiers, cabins of mud denoted not poverty so much as the conservatism that made them reluctant to depart from traditional building patterns. In co. Louth Young found that 'the common farmers, however, prefer living on the ground, surrounded by mud walls, have no idea of the chearfulness of large windows, but let in barely light enough to do their business through apertures not much better than loop holes'. Wakefield, finding farmers in co. Meath 'so wedded to their old habits that they never contemplate a change . . .', asked a farmer 'why he did not get a better house. His reply was that "he should break his shins going upstairs".' Except among the very poor and the destitute, furniture was not unduly sparse. Young declared that he had been 'in a multitude of cabbins that had much useful furniture, and some even superfluous; chairs, tables, boxes, chests of drawers, earthen ware'.

In some respects life was free and easy. In the country's largest industry, linen, the great bulk of the weavers were independent workers who determined their own hours and pace of work. Weavers could easily take a day off, and Young described the weavers in co. Armagh as 'keeping packs of hounds, every man one, and joining; they hunt hares: a pack of hounds is never heard, but all the weavers leave their looms, and away they go after them by hundreds'. Even for the many workers who lived in the houses of their rural employers, life was often easy-going and discipline was tolerant of weaknesses. In the records of a business family at Comber, items such as 'March 5 1770 drunk' or 'May 4 sick after drink' are mentioned as a matter of course in the record of 'Robert Conn's absent days', while in another entry $1s\ 7\frac{1}{2}d$ was charged against Charles Fallown 'to buy coals but he hapned to lose it at the cards'. In such an easy-going atmosphere business was always followed by pleasure. After a fair in co. Galway, Coquebert de Montbret had noted in 1791: 'the day after the fair nothing to be heard in the streets but song and laughter; nothing to be seen but games'. Cock-fights and races also drew idle crowds from the small towns no less than from the countryside. An estate agent in Lifford declared in 1758 that he 'wou'd allow neither cock-fight nor horse race though the people of the town were for it, as all towns are indeed....' Fairs and gatherings were sometimes the scene of less seemly proceedings: faction fights between different groups of peasants, divided by real or imagined

Rustic pastimes

Hurling match

grievance. A fight between several hundred persons took place at horse-races near Clonmel in 1771. In 1773 a man was killed in a row after a hurling match in Kilkenny. Coquebert de Montbret related in 1791 how 'three years ago, at a fair some miles from Portumna, two clans arranged a meeting a month beforehand. It was a matter of revenging an old man insulted by a young one. There were fifty against fifty.'

Athletic sports were popular. A young Tipperary boy studying for the priesthood on the Continent wrote wistfully of boyhood pastimes:

> Each day we were free to jump and to hunt,
> To play hurling and run races after swimming awhile,
> Driving the ball on the smooth, soft moorland,
> Farewell with a pang to that playtime.

Hurling matches took place between teams representing different baronies, the players on each team being distinguished by different colours in their caps. 'In these matches', according to Young, 'they perform such feats of activity, as ought to evidence the food they live on to be far from deficient in nourishment.' Swimming had long been a pastime of the young. But in the eighteenth century sea-bathing, little resorted to before this time, became fashionable. The accounts of the Andrew's of Comber in the second half of the century include the item '1½ yd of Green baze at 2s 2d thread ½d Miss Andrews for a bathing shift'. De Latocnaye in the course of his tour of Ireland described Tramore as 'one of the most remarkable places in Ireland, on account of the idlers, who assemble there, to bathe in the sea'. In Galway 'they flock in here from every corner of Connaught, on pretence of sea-bathing'. He related how 'in the morning, five or six young ladies, stowed in a car, with their legs hanging out, go two miles from the city to refresh their charms in the sea'.

There was of course a dark side to life also, even for those whose economic resources were not insufficient. Disease was common, although epidemics of disease abated in the course of the century. But the dreaded small-pox still killed or disfigured many. In Dublin many hospitals were established. But with only a little knowledge of the causes of infection, the hospitals killed as well as cured. Outside the capital, county infirmaries began to appear. But they were small, and can barely have touched the fringe of the huge problem of illness and disease. An estate agent's description of the new hospital in Omagh in 1767 gives an idea of what a contemporary hospital in county towns in Ireland was like: 'I went through the several apartments, and enquired at the patients, in what manner they were treated; they declared they were regularly attended by the surgeon and that they wanted for nothing, that they beleived was fitt for them . . . there has been 12 patients turned out, 10 of them recovered and two deemed incurable; there are 9 in the hospital, three of them to go out and four on the books to be admitted, as of last week.' Mortality rates were especially high among the very young. They were appalling in particular in the Foundling Hospital in Dublin, the death-rate among the children entrusted to its care horrifying even the not very squeamish minds of contemporaries.

The cottiers were but one element of rural society. Paid part in kind, part in cash, they were the manual labour force of the countryside. Their employers were the farmers, large and small, who were the dominant element. Small though many of their farms were, and badly housed though they often were, they had some capital. Young thought the capital of Irish farmers deficient by English standards, but each farmer was the owner of some livestock, draught animals, farm implements, ploughs and carts. In the poorer areas farmers took large farms in partnership, pooling the capital necessary to work the land. In the more prosperous areas dairy-farmers provided their own livestock. In poorer areas they rented the cows along with the land from a middleman, but enjoyed some improvement in their living standard where the rent was paid in cash and the dairyman stood to gain from the sharp rise in the price of butter from the middle of the century. But in remote and backward areas, where the rent continued to be paid in kind, the middleman and not the dairyman gained from the rise in prices, and the latter made only a bare living. Overall the farmers improved their conditions in the eighteenth century. They were able to spend money not only on conventional necessities like whiskey and tobacco but on new and fashionable products such as tea. Around Gorey, for instance, Young found 'no tea in the labourers' cabbins, but in those of little farmers they have it, and it increases much'.

Bathing and bathing-boxes on the shore at Ringsend

The cottier's condition was in sharp contrast to the tenant farmer's. Whereas the latter experienced real want only in the worst years of the century, the cottier remained at subsistence level even in good times. Poverty was his normal lot. Economic dependence on the farmer who gave him work was reflected in a low valuation of his labour and in a deferential attitude which accepted on occasion very high-handed treatment from his employer. But low though his condition was, the picture of social depression should not be painted too darkly. Extremely high-handed behaviour, such as an agent or landlord wantonly striking a cottier out of his way with a whip, did in fact take place. But in Young's words 'to accept that all these cases are common would be an exaggeration'. More serious in its implications for the cottier was his weak economic situation. He held his plot of land at the whim of the landowner, middleman, or more commonly farmer who employed him. His rent, though expressed in money, was often paid in labour. He was thus doubly vulnerable. His rent, which could be raised without difficulty, tended to rise if prices were rising or the demand for land becoming more acute. At the same time the low valuation put on his labour services was slow to change even when prices generally were going up. Cottiers themselves were not a single homogeneous class. Many rented land from an employer. If employment were regular these were the most secure of their class, and their wage income in conjunction with the sale of a calf or a pig left the family with a small cash surplus after rent had been allowed for. There were others, however, who rented a plot for cash, and sought employment from any source available. These were the worst off among the cottiers. They paid inflated rents for an acre or half-acre of potato ground, and unlike other cottiers whose employers provided grazing for a cow at a moderate charge (although in Young's opinion in some instances the cow may have been so poorly kept as to make the charge unreasonable), they had to buy milk from farmers in the locality. Both sorts of cottiers were sometimes in competition for the same work. Among the illiterate cottiers in the coal-mining area of Castlecomer, who signified by their mark on a document their 'determination to go to work whenever Lord Castlecomer calls upon us', there were some who held land from him 'provided we work with him and for him on the above mentioned terms', and others who held no land and were only offered 'all the incouragement proper'.

In one of his poems Eoghan Ruadh O'Súilleabháin threatened to go to Galway where wages were 6d. This apparently was regarded by him as a high rate and in fact in the late 1770s Young calculated the average wage as $6\frac{1}{2}d$ a day, having risen by $1\frac{3}{4}d$ in the preceding 20 years. In areas near the towns, where employment was plentiful, wages tended to be relatively high, and in more remote areas, where employment off the land was very scarce, they fell below the average. In some areas, as for instance near Listowel, wages were still as low as 4d a day in the slack winter months in the late 1770s. In better-developed areas the demand for labour in industry injected some buoyancy into the labour market. In Comber, co. Down, for instance,

Spinning and reeling linen yarn

even in 1760 the lowest rate of pay was 8*d* and in 1796 a labourer working on the farm received 10*d*, and when reaping 13*d*. Labourers' wages were much lower than in England. On the other hand, the wages of skilled workers were as high, sometimes higher, in Ireland. In the more backward areas, not only were labourers' wages low, but the absence of industry meant that there were little prospects of employment in spinning for women and children, which in some districts was an important addition to the income of the family. In linen-spinning areas, for instance, women might earn as much as $3\frac{1}{4}d$ a day in the 1770s, and a child of seven years 1*d* a day. In the south of Ireland, in parts where wool-spinning was prevalent, women and children might earn $1\frac{3}{4}d$ or 2*d* a day. Where such employment was not available, De Latocnaye's generalization that 'the price of his labour scarce suffices to maintain him and his family; the price of provisions is trebled, yet the price of labour remains the same', aptly describes the position of cottier families in the late 1790s.

As wage labour was not always to be found locally, some

cottiers migrated seasonally in search of work, especially in the harvest season when a general labour shortage and rising wages made outside labour welcome. An agent in Lifford in 1761 had declared that 'I shall stop doing any more 'till after the harvest, wages is so high, at 9*d* per day, if the weather be good, bad, or indifferent'. Migrant workers must be distinguished from the beggars who were equally numerous and who like the migrant

Peasantry – the market

labourers emerged intermittently or for longer periods from the cottier class. In some instances a cottier family resorted to begging while the father moved onwards as a migrant labourer. Poor and care-worn, the migrant workers left no record of their lives. We could not hope to see their lives through the eyes of one of their number, but for the fact that a peasant-poet from Munster, Eoghan Ruadh O'Súilleabháin, 'Eoghan an bhéil bhinn' or 'Eoghan the sweet-mouthed', left a record in the form of his poems. Eoghan was literate, and his life alternated between schoolmastering and migrant labour in the south of Ireland. From his poems we learn of his wanderings in the southern counties, of hard work with a spade, recurrent pennilessness, his illegitimate son, pretty girls and drinking bouts. Eoghan was young (he died at 36), irresponsible, liked company, and had apparently a talent and presence that appealed to many. Few of the workers can have taken to their lowly work and hard wandering with their small earnings sewn into their waistcoat with the same relish.

Some cottiers threw up hovels made of sods on waste ground or on the roadside. These were the most wretched of all, and their homes were also the worst, like, as one contemporary put it, 'birds' nests, of dirt wrought together and a few sticks and some straw, and like them are generally removed once a year'. If there was an able-bodied member of the family, some income from intermittent work done locally or as a migrant might relieve the family's plight. But in many instances the father was ill, or the hovel belonged to a widow with a family. Such families were quite numerous. In the early 1790s one-seventh of the families were exempt from the Hearth Tax either because they had no income or because there was no bread-winner. Most of these families were in the countryside, their hovels accumulating along the sides of the roads especially, and their misery was all the greater because, in contrast to England, there was no Poor Law to succour them.

The cottiers were generally cheerful and good-humoured. Arthur Young commented on their 'vivacity and a great and eloquent volubility of speech', and noted the popularity everywhere of dancing and the presence of itinerant dancing-masters, to whom cottiers paid 6d a quarter for dancing instruction. Instruction in music sometimes had an economic aspect. A peasant woman in 1767 told the English traveller, Samuel Derrick, of her eldest boy, Donagh, blinded by the small-pox, for whom 'we have got a man to teach him the bagpipes, with which and begging there is no fear, thank God, but he may get an honest livelihood and live very comfortably'. Anthony Raftery, the blind peasant-poet, though often as he said, 'playing music to empty pockets', maintained himself as an itinerant fiddler and by chronicling his own thoughts and the happenings that affected a peasant world, became a well-known figure

Turf footers

and something of an institution in early nineteenth-century Connaught.

Vagrancy, begging and charity were often the only recourse for the worst off. Beggars crowded into the towns, and also congregated during the season in provincial centres or in Killarney, already a tourist attraction for the well-to-do. Their extreme importunity often alienated both residents and visitors. Some were not impressed by their abject appearance: according to Swift 'their rags are part of the tools with which they work'. Even the lively and gay French traveller, De Latocnaye, 'never felt less inclined to be charitable than whilst in Dublin'. From the very moment that they landed on Irish soil, visitors could not but notice the large number of beggars. Significantly, they commented not only on their number, but on their abject condition, which compared unfavourably with that of beggars elsewhere.

Cottier's cabin

LIFE IN THE EIGHTEENTH CENTURY

Despite much poverty, cottiers and those with even less stake in the country had never dominated rural Ireland. A sharp rise in their number in the late eighteenth century was, however, an early sign of the grave crisis than in less than two generations was to engulf much of the Irish countryside.

Further Reading

J. C. Beckett, *The making of modern Ireland*, 1966
D. Corkery, *The hidden Ireland*, 1956
P. J. Dowling, *The hedge schools of Ireland*, 1935
I. Grubb, *Quakers in Ireland, 1654–1900*, 1927
M. McNeill, *The life and times of Mary Ann McCracken, 1770–1866*, 1960
C. Maxwell, *The stranger in Ireland*, 1954
—— *Dublin under the Georges, 1714–1830*, 1937
—— *Town and country in Ireland under the Georges*, 1949
D. O'Sullivan, *Carolan; The life, times and music of an Irish harper* (2 vols), 1958
J. G. Simms, 'Connacht in the eighteenth century', in *Irish Historical Studies*, vol. XI, no. 42, 1958
—— 'County Sligo in the eighteenth century' in *Journal of the Royal Society of Antiquaries of Ireland*, vol. XCI, pt. ii, 1961
M. Wall, *The penal laws, 1691–1760*, 1961
A. Young, *Tour in Ireland* (2 vols, ed. A. W. Hutton, 1892)
L. M. Cullen, 'The hidden Ireland: re-assessment of a concept', *Studia hibernica*, no. 9 (1969)
E. M. Johnston, *Ireland in the eighteenth century*, 1974

VI
Rural Crisis

Much of the promise of betterment in the eighteenth century was to be undone by a rural crisis whose first signs were already evident in the late eighteenth century. Over-population had not been a problem in most of the century. Poverty, and there had been much of it, had been largely due either to harvest failure or, in years when the country was free from the spectre of want, to low prices. Price trends for agricultural products from the 1740s were favourable to the seller. This greatly relieved the poverty which had so often been evident even amid plenty. Moreover, when harvests failed large imports of grain staved off famine and prevented a repetition of the famines of 1728-29 and 1740-41.

The country's population had been relatively stable in the first half of the eighteenth century. But its growth accelerated from the middle of the century. The reasons for this significant demographic change are not quite clear. Possibly a better diet consequent on a more generous and continuous supply of foodstuffs helped to reduce mortality. Fever, the aftermath of hunger or undernourishment, was also apparently less prevalent. Marriages, too, may have been more frequent. The reasons are, however, a matter of speculation. The only certainty is the fact that population grew more rapidly.

A larger population in rural Ireland necessarily meant greater competition for land. This was reflected in a disproportionate rise in the number of people renting minute plots of land, because their small substance and lack of capital prevented them from being seriously considered by a landlord as prospective tenants. These people were the cottiers, renting small plots, mostly from tenant farmers, paid in labour services or out of a precarious income as day-labourers. The land let to cottiers tended to be the land least attractive or convenient for commercial farming. Cottiers' plots were generally found on the least convenient parts of a farm. Their holdings as a whole were in consequence most likely to be found in the inferior uplands above good farming land, and, in the country at large, in the poorer regions where low returns in commercial farming made it easier for cottiers to acquire land. As early as the 1770s the evidence of population growth was already impressive. At Castle Oliver in co. Limerick, according to Arthur Young, 'the population of the country increases exceedingly, but most in the higher lands; new cabbins are building everywhere'. In the barony of Tyreragh in co. Sligo, he noted that 'they increase in number very greatly so as to be evidently crowded'. In the bleak lands around Westport the numbers on Lord Altamont's estate had doubled in 20 years.

The tenant farmers, possessing leases for their holdings, were protected against the worst consequences of sharper competition for land. Although rents on new leases rose sharply after mid-century, the farmers could count on an unchanging rent during a period of 21 or 31 years, or even longer, while the prices realized for their produce rose sharply at the same time. The cottiers were a stark contrast. The rent of their plots was not restrained by a long-term agreement. rents could rise from one year to the next. The rise in the wage rates of labourers between the 1750s and the 1770s was in large measure offset by the rise in the rents of small plots. This was, however, a period of rapid expansion in agricultural output, and the cottier stood to gain at least by more regular employment. At Slane in co. Meath a landlord informed Young that 20 years previously 'if he gave notice at the mass-houses, that he wanted labourers, in two days he could have 2 or 300; now it is not so easy to get 20, from the quantity of regular employment being so much increased'.

There was in consequence no general worsening in the cottiers' condition between these two dates. But in some regions, where the cottier population was relatively large or the land poor, the condition of the people had deteriorated in these years. This, according to Young, was the position in co. Kerry and in parts of co. Westmeath. In some other areas they had barely held their own. As population continued to expand, deterioration became more general and more serious. It was reflected in the rising disparity of rents between commercial farming and subsistence land. On one large estate in 1844 rents paid by tenants averaged £1 2s 2d net per acre; cottiers' rents, £4 16s 5d. Moreover, rents in commercial farming fell in 1815 and did not subsequently recover vigorously. Cottiers' rents continued to rise. The rent of conacre land, i.e. land hired for a single season, was the most sensitive barometer of the growing competition among cottiers. The rent of conacre in the late 1770s, according to Young, averaged £3, rising as high as £6 or higher in the vicinity of the larger towns. By the mid-1840s conacre rents varied from £4 on inferior lands to as high as £10 or £12 per acre near towns. The holder of a minute farm in co. Monaghan related to the Devon Commission in the 1840s how his rent had recently been raised from £3 19s 11d to £5 19s 9d.

The labour market in no way expanded proportionately with the upsurge in population after the 1770s. With the fall in agricultural prices after 1815, farmers tended if anything to economize on hired labour. Moreover, with more farmers competing for land, farm sizes were smaller than previously, and dependence on family as opposed to

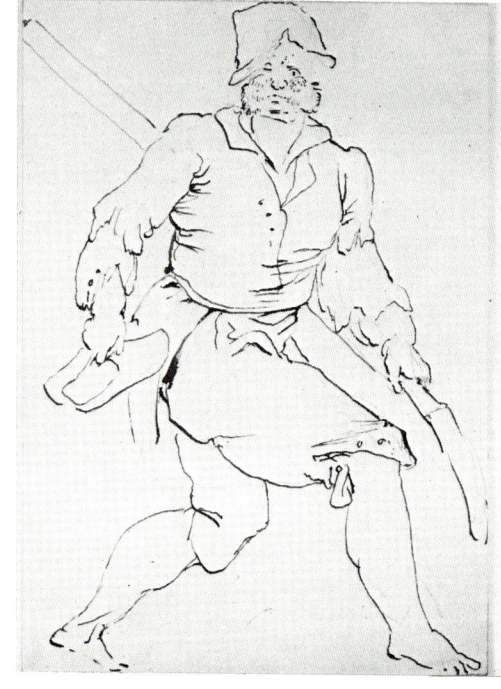

Peasant with spade and shoes in hand

hired labour greater. Competition for available employment ensured that, despite the rise in rents, there was no compensating rise in wage rates. In Connaught and in the south-west wages in the 1840s were at 6*d* to 8*d* a day scarcely higher than they had been 50 years previously; and elsewhere they were only 8*d* to 10*d*. Cottiers, holding a plot whose rent was paid off in labour to a tenant farmer, were in a favoured position. The annual income of such a labourer, assured of regular employment, might amount to £8 to £16, and his rent deducted he received a net cash balance from his employer. An increasing number of peasants, however, had to take conacre land at inflated rents, and sought to sell their services to any employer. Most of these could hope only to secure intermittent employment: as early as 1830 only a third of the rural labourers could count on permanent employment. In conjunction with inflated rents, under-employment and low rates for what days they worked made their plight desperate. The sale of a pig fattened on potatoes or of poultry helped to compensate for the lack of a regular income. The large number of pigs and poultry in rural Ireland in the early nineteenth century was a new feature, and the sharp rise in their number at this time reflected the pressing need of many cottiers to supplement their scant incomes.

Pig-drover

But such supplementary income was far from sufficient for many, especially in the more remote areas or on poorer lands. Migrant labour, far from unknown in these areas in the eighteenth century, was now becoming a more common feature. Seasonally labourers migrated from Connaught to the more prosperous parts of Leinster. Labourers from Kerry and west Cork went to Waterford or Limerick, attracted by wages of 8*d* a day and their food. But with growing population even within the prosperous areas, the seasonal migrant himself had to face resentment in the areas which had traditionally employed migrant labour. Migrants were, for instance, attacked by local labourers in the Decies region of co. Waterford, and in 1835 a labourer from co. Kerry told a commission of enquiry that 'the wretched pittance they earn, to pay for the conacres at home, is not only purchased by the sweat of their brow, but by their blood also, and the risk of their lives, as they are wantonly, cruelly, and most barbarously treated by the natives for their intrusion'.

In such circumstances an increasing number of migrants were tempted by the English and Scottish haymaking and harvest seasons. The number of seasonal migrants rose from some 6,000 to 8,000 in the 1820s to 57,651 in 1841. Having arrived in Britain, the labourers tramped the countryside in search of work, or, as in the case of many going to Scotland, stood daily at the hiring fair beside Glasgow Green until some farmer employed them. The seasonal migrant, if he remained for the harvest after the haymaking, might bring home £3 to £5. The exact numbers returning, it was impossible to enumerate, because 'on their return to Ireland, they land in such haste, that all attempts to count them were abandoned'.

A predominantly potato diet was not common in the

Labourer

eighteenth century. Except for the very poor, the potato was only a subsidiary foodstuff. But as population grew, dependence on the potato became more marked especially among the cottiers and generally in the more remote areas, where competition for arable land was most acute. Housing also deteriorated, the worst houses like the potato diet occurring in the areas or social

Peasant with hayfork

classes in which population pressure was most evident. The Commissioners for the 1841 Census divided housing into four categories, the fourth or lowest consisting of cabins, mostly of mud, having one room only. Some 40 per cent of the houses consisted of such houses, but though they existed in every part of Ireland, they were most numerous in the west generally. In over-populated districts in these areas, such houses might account for 60 or even 75 per cent of the housing. The next category of houses consisted of houses having two to four rooms and windows. These houses accounted for 37 per cent of Irish housing. They were generally built of mud, but this did not necessarily denote poverty: they represented an older tradition of house-building with the use of traditional materials and less account taken of the growing desire for space and privacy within the family. But in the most advanced areas a considerable proportion of the houses had five or more rooms, often built of stone. East of a line from Cork to Dublin and in east Ulster, 20–40 per cent of the houses consisted of such structures.

In the poorest areas and in the poorest homes furniture was in keeping with the wretched structures. At Derrynane Bog in

Kerry, for instance, in 1845 'the distress of the people was horrible. There is not a pane of glass in the parish, nor a window of any kind in half the cottages. Some have got a hole in the wall for light, with a board to stop it up. In not one in a dozen is there a chair to sit upon, or anything whatever in the cottages beyond an iron pot and a rude bedstead with some straw on it; and not always that. In many of them the smoke is coming out the doorway, and they have no chimneys . . . the poor creatures are in the lowest degree of squalid poverty.' In the parish of West Tullaghobegley in north-west Donegal a few years earlier conditions were if anything worse: there were said to be only 10 beds, 93 chairs, and 243 stools among 9,000 people. Clothing was in keeping with diet and housing. In 1845 a correspondent of the London *Times* noted that 'in the west I never saw a woman below the rank of lady, or in towns below that of a shopkeeper's wife, who wore stockings and shoes . . . in the county of Wexford I have not seen any woman not decently clad with stockings and shoes.'

Sub-division of holdings was becoming prevalent in poorer regions: tenants split up farms as a means of providing for their families, or tempted by the profits of conacre rents offered by other peasants. Lord Monteagle had told the economist Nassau Senior that 'the Irish tenant is not to be trusted with a lease. His instinct is while he is alive to sublet the land, in order to have an income without trouble and on his death to divide it among his children.' The progress of sub-division in Leinster and in the prosperous regions in Munster was limited by the interest of tenant and landlord alike in commercial farming. The fact that land in poor areas was often held in partnership between peasants under the rundale system facilitated sub-division: sons and relatives easily acquired a stake in the land, and as population grew the landlord had less and less knowledge of the actual occupiers. The rundale system was beginning to break up in the early nineteenth century, but under the pressure of population growth the process of sub-division, little restrained by commercial farming, was proceeding far in these areas. Menlough, a rundale village of 2,000 inhabitants, a mile or two from Galway, as described by the correspondent of

The Times in 1845, typifies the society of such areas: 'as this is the largest village I ever saw, so it is the poorest, the worst built, the most strangely irregular, and the most completely without head or centre, or market or church, or school, of any village I ever was in. It is an overgrown democracy. No man is better or richer than his neighbour in it.' Of the 685,309 holdings of upwards of an acre in 1841, 45 per cent were between one and

Barefooted girl in cottage interior, west Galway

five acres; in Connaught, the most sub-divided of the provinces, the proportion rose to 64 per cent. Moreover, the number of families dependent on agriculture—974,188—was larger than the number of holdings (685,309). Some of these extra families may have occupied the holdings of less than an acre, estimated at 135,134 in 1841, but many of them must have had no land or simply a tenuous right to occupancy of a plot on other holdings.

In the northern half of the country especially, many families had supplemented their earnings in agricultural employment by spinning or weaving. But in many areas such opportunities were limited. Moreover, with the advent of factory spinning in the north-east in the 1820s, rural spinners of linen yarn were unable to compete effectively, and many families lost a valuable supplement to their incomes. Even in weaving, although power-loom weaving was not introduced in this period, weavers close to Belfast had an advantage over those in other areas. Concentration of weaving on the north-east, already evident, became more marked. Life had become more precarious for a growing number of people in rural Ireland. Beggars also had become more numerous in the countryside and in town. Travellers related how coaches were importuned by begging children on their routes, and George Nicholls, one of the architects of the Irish Poor Law in the late 1830s, commented that 'a mass of filth, nakedness and squalor, is kept roaming about the country, entering every house, addressing itself to every eye, and soliciting from every hand'.

Competition for land, as it sharpened, was bound to result in increased resentments among peasants themselves. The factions, and the fights they often led to, frequently had some such origin. 'I never knew them attack anyone for money', said a Tipperary merchant, 'but touch the farm and turn them out and they get frantic and wild.' The Whiteboys in Munster, so called because on their nocturnal expeditions of intimidation they sometimes covered themselves with white smocks, were the most widespread sign of such unrest in the 1760s. Sporadic and isolated though its stirrings were, and meeting with firm resistance from the magistrates and the gentry, it continued into the 1780s. The Oakboys and Steelboys were contemporary manifestations of unrest in the north.

Some of the grievances of these movements were unrelated to the possession of land. For instance, resentment at the cess levied for road-building was behind the Oakboy movement, and the tithes paid to the Church of Ireland were a grievance common to agrarian societies in most areas. But tensions arising from greater competition for land were already a prime cause of organized unrest. The Whiteboy movement had originally been sparked off by the enclosure of common land, and hostility was also vented against outsiders who came into an area to take farms at higher rents. In the north the general competition for land was exacerbated by religious differences between Catholic and Presbyterian tenants. Feuds originally caused by agrarian grievances easily developed along sectarian lines. Catholic homes were raided by Peep O'Day Boys for arms. In turn Catholics began to band together in local groups of Defenders, which were loosely affiliated with one another. Religious tension led to the foundation of the Orange Order in 1795 in the north to protect Protestant interests. Growing tensions in the north facilitated the spread of the Defender movement into Leinster because of the fears of religious conflict, exaggerated but to the peasant appearing very real, they aroused. The 1798 Rebellion, widespread in co. Wexford among the peasantry, led to exaggerated reports in the reverse direction, inflaming the fears of Protestants in the north still further. From this time the line dividing Protestants and Catholics in the north, and the north and south generally became very pronounced. The United Irishmen movement, the revolutionary body offering brotherhood to all Irishmen, had been first espoused by radical northern Presbyterians, but after the 1798 Rebellion support for it in the north, at the time widespread, melted away. It was the last body offering hope of bridging the rising religious gulf, characteristic of modern Ireland.

Farmer and child

Among the peasantry the revolutionary ideals of the 1790s, despite the contacts with the Defenders developed by the United Irishmen, hardly ran deep. Local societies of Ribbonmen, cherishing republican aspirations, were fairly widespread in the first half of the nineteenth century. But their membership was stronger in the towns than in the countryside, consisting of artisans, carters, schoolmasters rather than of farmers and labourers. Agrarian unrest remained concerned with practical aims. Agrarian secret societies were in fact more prevalent in the nineteenth century than in the past, resort to violence more common, and the efforts of the authorities, though determined, less successful. The hostility of these societies was directed not so much against landlords, who were often popular among their tenantry, as against other peasants, especially outsiders, who took farms over the heads of local farmers. This unrest was largely absent from Ulster and from Connaught (Leitrim excepted), because sub-division offered easy access for all to what land there was, but was endemic in rich agricultural areas such as Tipperary and Limerick. In these areas commercial farming ensured that holdings were harder to acquire than elsewhere. It is significant that although in Kerry and west Cork conditions were akin to Connaught and Donegal, yet taking Munster as a whole the disparity between the number of holdings and the number of families engaged in agriculture was larger than in the other provinces— in 1841 some 285,000 occupied on a total of 162,000 holdings of an acre or more. This was the basis of acute competition for land, and for peasants courting the resentment of land-hungry local men by bidding for farms outside their own parish. It is sometimes said that a demand for tenant-right, that is for some legally recognized permanent stake in a holding, led to this unrest. The reverse would be truer. The demand for tenant-right grew out of the swell of unrest as an answer to competition which was creating an altogether novel degree of uncertainty.

Improvements in communications were rapid in this period. In fact, by opening up the more remote areas, they were responsible for revealing to the outside world areas whose poverty could not be paralleled in the rest of the country. Connemara, much of Mayo, Donegal and Kerry were almost completely isolated before this. As late as 1834 the traveller, Inglis, remarked of Donegal: 'there is evidently a want of everything necessary to improvement; encouragement, capital, and above all, the great preliminary, facilities of communication'. In 1802 it has been stated of co. Tyrone that 'about 20 years

Emigrants on the Quays, Cork, c. 1840

ago, very few wheel-cars were to be met with, except in the neighbourhood of principal towns, such as Dungannon, Omagh and Strabane'. In a good year peasants could not hope to dispose of surplus grain: this was said to be one reason for the prevalence of illicit distilling in these areas. After a bad harvest, supplies could not readily be brought in from outside, and in consequence suffering in isolated areas was on occasion far more appalling than elsewhere. However, road-building proceeded very rapidly in the early nineteenth century. Already, after the 1798 Rebellion, a great military road had been built across the Wicklow Mountains. From 1822 parliamentary grants were available to help road-building, and from 1832 the Board of Works itself executed road-works in the more remote areas. Between 1834 and 1845, 233 miles of road were made in Kerry, 140 by the Board of Works. A Scottish engineer, Nimmo, was responsible for opening up Connemara, and Galway was now linked with the westernmost parts of the county by the great road from Galway to Clifden. Another road, the Antrim Coast Road, linked together the various Antrim glens. A Board of Works road from Malins to the Gweedore River in 1834 was the first road through the Donegal Mountains.

(*overleaf*) *Street scene: stage-coach, 1820*

The roads brought considerable change to these areas. When a new road had been built at Iveragh in co. Kerry, for instance, 'the old inhabitants of the hill left their cabins and built new ones along the new road sides'. Trade followed. According to a 1838 report 'even small portions of those roads were scarcely out of the engineers' hands before they were covered with the carts of the farmers, eager to take advantage of the improvement.' Small towns began to grow at focal points on these roads such as Clifden, Roundstone, Cahirciveen and Belmullet. On the busier roads coach services were quickly established: the coach service to Cahirciveen began in 1836 and that to Clifden in the following year. In 1842 Thackeray travelled as far as Ballynahinch, home of the Martins, on the Clifden mail-car. Only the most intrepid of travellers had ventured into Connemara previously. Tourists were now beginning to make their acquaintance with the region, and as early as 1841 Leenane was reported to have a good inn.

With the improvement in roads, evident in developed areas as in remote areas, went a great increase in travel facilities. In 1811 there were only about ten mail-coach routes; in 1842 there were 22 services covering 2,000 miles a day. Better roads resulted in greater speeds. By the early 1840s coaches averaged nine miles an hour. Coaching was now at its peak. The railways were still in their infancy. In the 1841 Census only 25 persons were returned as railway employees, and in 1845 only seventy miles of railway were open to traffic. Thackeray, crossing the midlands to Dublin, travelled with a 'clergyman, a guard, a Scotch farmer, a butcher, a bookseller's hack, a lad bound for Maynooth and another for Trinity...'. In 1834 John O'Donovan, working for the Ordnance Survey, took a coach named the *Fair Trader* from Derry to Enniskillen, 'carrying about 28 passengers, ten inside and 18 on the outside—noisy and half inebriated fellows'. Competition from the coaching services forced the canals to introduce in the 1830s faster boats, named flyboats. In 1836 the Grand Canal carried 101,000 passengers, the Royal Canal 46,000. In addition to coach services, commuter services were appearing around the large towns. Twelve cars went from Carrickfergus to Belfast and back every day as

Taking up a passenger

early as 1827. Moreover, after 1815, the deficiency in cross-services between the main routes was being remedied by the emergence of coaching services operating a whole network of routes. The most famous of these concerns was established by an Italian immigrant, Bianconi, who ran his first car between Clonmel and Cahir in 1815. His services expanded rapidly, covering 1,800 miles and 23 centres by 1832 and 3,800 miles and 120 centres by 1845. These services, charging $1\frac{1}{2}d$ per mile, were cheap enough to be of great benefit to rural areas. As Bianconi himself said in 1843: 'the farmer who formerly drove and spent three days in making his market, can now do so in one for a few shillings; thereby saving two clear days and the expense of his horses'.

Tourist traffic was growing as well. It encouraged the appearance of better inns. Thackeray, for instance, spoke well of Irish inns, and at Killarney, of whose inns complaints had once been many, the German visitor, Von Puckler-Muskau, reported in 1828 that 'incessant resort of English tourists has almost introduced into the inns an English elegance and English prices'. The main tourist attractions were now well established—in particular Killarney and Glendalough, both well supplied with guides and boatmen for the benefit of the tourist, and the Giant's Causeway. A branch of tourism which attracted local people to the seaside was sea-bathing, now becoming very popular. Small resorts were growing along the coast to serve the towns or the prosperous agricultural hinterland. Blackrock, co. Louth, according to Lewis in 1837, was 'much frequented, during the summer seasons, by the farmers of the inland counties, both for the purposes of bathing and drinking the sea-water'. Tramore in the south-east already had a hotel and several boarding-houses, attracting for several weeks shopkeepers and their families from Waterford.

Good communications of themselves did not alter the rural character of Ireland. In fact, by facilitating intercourse and widening the hinterland of the larger towns, they enhanced their importance at the expense of smaller towns. Of a population of 8,175,124 enumerated in the 1841 Census, only 1,135,465 lived in towns of 2,000 and upwards. There were in all only 18 towns with a population in excess of 10,000: of these only five exceeded 20,000. Moreover, Cork, Waterford and Limerick expanded only slowly, and even Dublin's population increased from only 200,000 in 1800 to 232,726 in 1841. Belfast, expanding from 18,320 in 1791 to 75,308 in 1841, was exceptional. In 1841 80 per cent of the population lived in isolated houses or in communities of 20 houses or less. Where country towns grew, it was often simply because growing poverty in the countryside pushed many into the towns or their fringes in search of casual employment. Of the 881 families in Bantry in 1841, only 400 were in regular employment. Fifty families lived from begging, and the remainder from the returns of a garden and the sale of a pig or by collecting seaweed from the shore. Such families lived in appalling conditions. In Kells in co. Meath in 1836, for instance, 'a number of these cabins are situated in little courts at the back of the main row of cabins which form the front of the street or road. These courts are seldom more than six or seven feet wide, and that space, which

View of Kells, 1819

Elephant in the Dublin Zoological Gardens

forms the only passage or entrance to the cabins, is usually blocked up with the heaps of manure made by the pigs, and with the rubbish and filth thrown out of the houses at the very doors.'

The Union between Ireland and England in 1801 did not immediately alter the character of Dublin. Nine years after the union some 40 peers still lived in or near Dublin. Moreover, the presence of a large and still growing commercial and professional class in large measure made good the loss of the city's political life as a capital to London. Impressive buildings such as St George's Church and the General Post Office were built in this period. Mountjoy Square was finished only in 1818 and Fitzwilliam Square in 1825. After 1830 house-building for the city's prosperous and expanding middle classes spilled out across the Grand Canal into new suburban areas. The city did not give an immediate impression of decline to the visitor, although belief in its decline was common among its citizens. In 1825 Sir Walter Scott had stated: 'they tell me the city is desolate of which I can see no appearance, but the deprivation caused by the retreat of the most noble and opulent inhabitants must be felt in a manner a stranger cannot conceive.'

The contrast between well-to-do and poor areas was, however, if anything sharper than before. The crowded quarter of the 'liberties' suffered both by the decline of many of its artisanal industries and by the move of the city's centre to the

William Belcher, M.D. and family with Miss Jane Waring

east. Thackeray in 1843 noted of the district's main street, Thomas Street, 'we passed through a street which was thriving once, but has fallen since into a sort of a decay, to judge outwardly'. Engels in 1844 wrote that 'the poor quarters of Dublin are extremely extensive, and the filth, the uninhabitableness of the houses and the neglect of the streets surpass all description.' Evidence of this poverty flowed into other districts in the form of beggars and the 'troops of dirty children' commented on by Thackeray.

Mulholland's Linen Mill, Belfast, c. 1840

Most towns were similar to Dublin in that their importance was commercial rather than industrial. The poverty of their poorer areas was no less evident. Thackeray in describing Cork referred to 'alleys where the odours and rags and the darkness are so hideous, that one runs frightened away from them'.

Sedan-chair and bearers

Belfast was in striking contrast. The decline of its cotton-spinning mills was compensated by the rise of linen-mills of which there were 25 in 1841. It was rapidly becoming an industrial town. In 1836 50 of the 150 steam-engines in Ireland were in Belfast. In 1834 'on all sides are seen near and far, manufactories, or mills, as they are called, of immense extent, evidently newly erected. . . .' Thackeray related how 'the town was surrounded by huge spinning mills of which the thousand windows were lighted up at night, and could be seen from all quarters'.

From the end of the century Catholics had been free of the bulk of the restrictions which had affected them. Their growing confidence was reflected in the famous agitation led by Daniel O'Connell in the 1820s culminating in 1829 in Catholic Emancipation. Maynooth was established with the aid of a Government subsidy in 1795 as a seminary intended to enlarge the opportunities of completing an education for the priesthood and thus reduce foreign influences on the formation of the Catholic clergy. By 1845 half the bishops and nearly half the parish priests had been educated at Maynooth. The Catholic priests had already acquired a prominent place in rural life in Ireland, and had frequently emerged as local leaders of the people. The Church's visible strength became more evident in the first half of the century. The parish clergy increased by 50 per cent in this period, new seminaries were built and from the 1820s began a wave of church-building to replace the modest structures of the eighteenth century.

Although the number of schools was large and growing rapidly, attendance was often intermittent, schools themselves were still scarce in some regions, and the teaching was often of poor quality or its very provision irregular. While illiteracy was as low as 12 per cent in some of the baronies in the north-east, according to the 1841 Census, 85 to 90 per cent of the population aged five years and above was illiterate in the four western baronies of co. Galway. The Board of National Education, established in 1831 to provide assistance towards the cost of buildings and teachers' salaries, helped in educational progress. But the rapid rise in the number of schools coming under the Board in its first two decades in no small measure simply reflects the absorption into its system of already existing schools; many schools still declined to give up their independence, to accept its subsidies, and in any event school inspection and teacher training were still too limited to claim credit for the undoubted improvements in schooling in the nineteenth century. The teaching of Irish language and Irish history was

Interior of a Belfast linen-spinning mill

excluded from schools coming under the Board. Some independent schools offered these subjects, but in time many of these came under the Board of National Education. The exclusion of the Irish language from the schools quickened its decline.

Four hundred people at Mass kneeling round an ark at Kilbaha beach, 1857

In 1800 Irish was spoken by about half the population. West of a line from Cork to Derry the majority spoke Irish, and it remained a vigorous language, although the majority of its speakers were illiterate. By 1851, however, only a quarter of the population spoke Irish, and a mere five per cent were without some knowledge of English. The national schools were not the only factor contributing to the decline of the language. The middle classes, small but influential because of the growth of trade, were indifferent to it, and greater intercourse with outside areas only helped to undermine Irish in the districts in which it had been most deep rooted. English became the language of the popular political agitations, starting with O'Connell's great agitation for Emancipation in the 1820s. The Church itself was a vehicle of linguistic anglicization, and Archbishop MacHale was one of the few prominent churchmen to take an interest in the language. The use of Irish in the everyday life of literate families, as for instance in the case of the schoolmaster–shopkeeper, Amhlaoibh O'Súilleabháin of Callan, co. Kilkenny, keeping a diary in Irish of everyday events, was by now unusual. Even the spoken language was beginning to lose some of its vigour. Poets such as the Munster peasant-poets or in Connaught Anthony Raftery had no real successors, and the accumulated heritage of the past century remained alive on the lips of a steadily declining number of peasants.

The use of English by the literate, and the identification of

Irish with poverty which it led to, speeded the decline of the language still further.

The first half of the nineteenth century was a period of rapid change in administration, which not only affected the life of the people closely but had a striking physical embodiment in new building. Changes in urban administration were to give the towns more effective cleaning and lighting. Law and order were also better organized, a fact reflected in the building of court-houses and gaols in the 1820s. For the first time, a regular, full-time, national police force came into being in 1836 with the amalgamation of the peace preservation force or 'peelers' which since 1814 had operated in disaffected areas, and of the old-style and ineffective baronial police, into a force under an inspector-general, empowered to 'provide one uniform system of rules and regulations for the Irish police establishment'. The men were trained in a central depot, a uniform was provided and recruits were required to be 'of sound constitution, able to read and write and of a good character for honesty, fidelity and activity'. The new force was para-military in organization, and its police-stations—'barracks'—semi-fortified, became an essential feature of Irish life. Going by mail-car from Bantry to Kenmare in 1842, the German traveller, Kohl, related finding a police-station in a wild countryside, 'a little strong castle', reminiscent of a military post on the Austrian frontier.

Hospitals were also more numerous in Dublin and outside it. By 1843 there were 34 county hospitals, each with 30 to 70 beds. Fever hospitals also increased in number in the 1820s and 1830s. Hospitals added to the administrative importance of the towns, although their number was still too small and, in a rural society distances often too great, to put them within access of the mass of the people. As late as 1845 there were still several counties without a fever hospital. Even the dispensaries with doctor attached, of which in 1836 there were 500, were able to touch only the fringe of illness and suffering. They covered large areas, many areas had no dispensary and in the entire county of Mayo there was in 1836 only a single dispensary. The Poor Law, introduced into Ireland in the late 1830s,

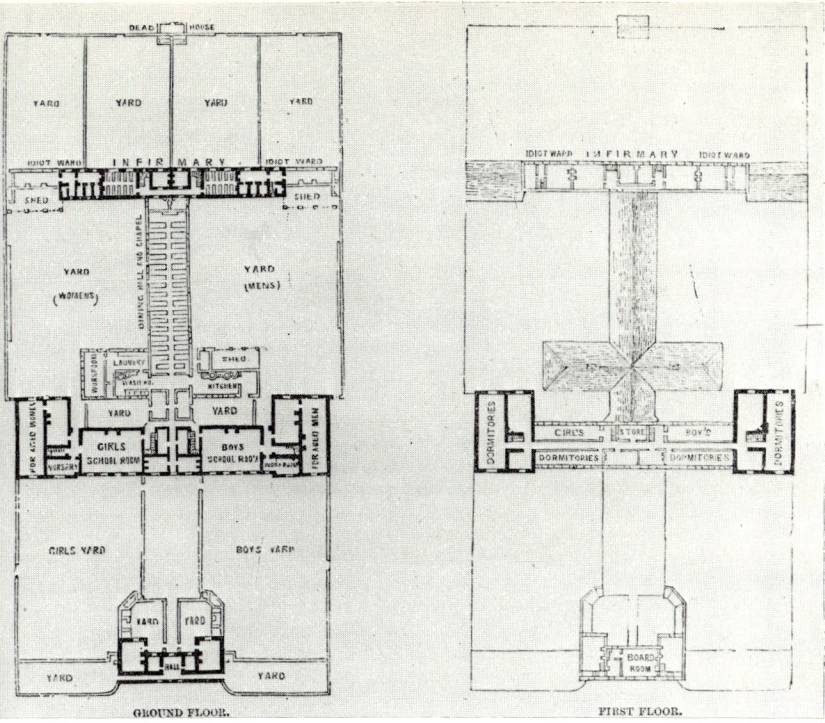

Plan of a workhouse

resulted in the building of a large number of workhouses, mostly on the outskirts of towns, but in areas where there was no focal urban centre, in the countryside. The gabled roofs, elongated chimneys and the mullioned windows of the workhouses, according to their architect Wilkinson, gave 'a pleasing and picturesque appearance', and if a few trees were planted around the building, 'the whole may be an ornament rather than the reverse to the neighbourhood'. The austere régime within the workhouses, however, probably made a greater impact, an intended one, on the mass of the people. To discourage all but the genuinely destitute, the Commissioners of the Poor Law were to rely on 'regularity, orderliness, strict enforcement of cleanliness, constant occupation, the preservation of decency and decorum, and the exclusion of all irregular habits and tempting excitements'.

Despite the poverty, the mass of the people were cheerful. According to Nicholls, the Poor Law organizer and expert, 'if

Dancing at a fair

there be a market to attend, a fair or a funeral, a horse race or a wedding, all else is neglected and forgotten'. The night before the races at Kilkenny, according to a traveller, the main street was crowded in every corner with 'bagpipes snuffling, violins squeaking, melancholy flutes blowing and ragged Paddies dancing'. But this teeming and lively society was now living in the shadow of disaster. An American woman who had visited Ireland in 1844 had already remarked that 'there must needs be an explosion of some kind or other'. And come one did. Partial failures of the potato crop had already occurred, resulting in minor famines. Fever accompanied famine and undernourishment. The consequences of a total failure of the potato crop were bound to be even more disastrous. Such failure occurred in three of the four years from 1845 to 1848, and fever carried off many more. Want was on such a scale that the administrative machinery of the age was unable to cope with it. The numbers receiving assistance testify to the scale of the disaster. In March 1847 over 700,000 were employed on public relief works. After the works were abandoned, the total number of people receiving food at Government soup kitchens daily had risen by August of the same year to three million. A million died from hunger, or more often from famine fever, in these years. Another million emigrated. Modern Ireland emerged from these years, a country with a declining population and a growing political embitterment.

Further Reading

J. Carty, *Ireland from Grattan's Parliament to the Great Famine*, 1965
K. H. Connell, *The population of Ireland, 1750–1845*, 1950
R. D. Edwards and T. D. Williams (ed.), *The Great Famine*, 1963
T. W. Freeman, *Pre-famine Ireland*, 1957
E. R. R. Green, *The Lagan Valley, 1800–1850*, 1949
B. M. Kerr, 'Irish seasonal migration to Great Britain, 1800–38', in *Irish Historical Studies*, vol. 3, no. 12, 1942–43
C. Maxwell, *The stranger in Ireland*, 1954
R. B. McDowell (ed.), *Social life in Ireland, 1800–45*, 1963
T. W. Moody and J. C. Beckett (ed.), *Ulster since 1800: a political and economic survey*, 1954
—— *Ulster since 1800: a social survey*, 1957
K. B. Nowlan, 'Agrarian unrest in Ireland, 1800–1845', *University Review*, vol. 2, no. 6, 1959
C. Woodham-Smith, *The Great Hunger*, 1962
L. M. Cullen, *An economic history of Ireland since 1660*, 1972
W. A. Maguire, *The Downshire estates in Ireland, 1801–1845*, 1972
G. O'Tuathaigh, *Ireland before the Famine 1798–1848*, 1972

VII

Post-Famine Ireland

The Famine is the most convenient dividing line in the history of rural Ireland in modern times. Within the decade 1841-51 the population fell by two million. Moreover, though emigration subsequently fell from the high level of the 1840s, it was to remain—together with late and relatively few marriages—an outstanding social feature of Ireland. From Famine times emigration was higher than the excess of births over deaths; it thus led to a continuing decline in population, decade after decade. By 1911 the island's population, compared with 1841, had been almost halved. Town population as a whole rose during this period. It was the countryside more than the towns which altered, and emigration was the solution because with the exception of Belfast, Dublin and Derry, few Irish towns expanded.

Over much of the country the cottier all but disappeared, and the decline in population made it possible to enlarge the holdings of tenant farmers. In 1851 the new agent of the Guinness estates in co. Wexford and co. Wicklow said that his intention was 'to negotiate the surrender of farms, put them into condition, drain and consolidate them with a view of letting them at some future period in large tracts to solvent and improving tenants'. Indebtedness among many landowners had been a factor inhibiting investment in agriculture. The sale in the 30 years following 1849 of some five million acres, almost a quarter of the area of Ireland, under the Encumbered Estates Act, by transferring land to less indebted owners, made possible investment in consolidation and drainage. The tenants of larger

Christmas morning in an Irish country shop: giving the customary presents

consolidated holdings were also sanguine about the prospects of a satisfactory return on investment in their holdings. Some English and Scottish farmers were even attracted to Ireland. In particular 'about the year 1850, after the Famine, large numbers of British farmers, as a speculation, hopefully rented large tracts of evicted land in the west, and proceeded to drain them'. The 1850s and 1860s were prosperous for Irish agriculture. A reduction in subsistence production admitted of a larger market surplus. Moreover, price trends favoured the farmer. A switch to grazing and dairying enabled farmers to take advantage of a sharp upward trend in the prices of cattle and butter. Even grain prices remained remarkably stable in this period. In consequence, though the area under grass and meadow increased, crop acreages did not contract sharply. In barley the acreage actually increased because of the prosperity of the brewing and distilling industries; the decline in the acreage of oats was little more than a fifth, and though wheat-growing declined more sharply, the acreage sown between 1855 and 1870 was still larger than the barley acreage. Landlord and tenant alike shared in the benefits.

But the evidence of prosperity should not be allowed to obscure the tensions which existed in the countryside. Social tensions leading to unrest and violence smouldered in the more prosperous counties. The prevalence of commercial farming limited access to land for landless men or for small farmers anxious to enlarge their holdings. Such resentment was on occasion, and especially in bad years, explosive. Moreover, consolidation of holdings in the post-Famine years was resented, and, where insolvent tenants were numerous and attempts to collect arrears determined, sometimes resulted in agrarian outrage and discontent. Unrest died down, however, as insolvent tenants departed and prices recovered. In co. Monaghan, for instance, which had been very agitated in the early 1850s, Steuart Trench, agent of the Bath estate in the barony of Farney, reported in 1868 that 'industry, order, punctuality in the payment of rents, and a desire for, and tendency towards improvement, are the general characteristics of the day'. However, the prosperity of commercial farming and the vulnerability, as revealed in the Famine years, of the areas of minute and largely subsistence farms led some landlords in the backward areas of the country to attempt to reduce the numbers of small holdings as a prelude to the introduction of a more highly commercialized agriculture. Where such attempts were made, agrarian outrage followed. And if it did not become general in these areas, it was because few landlords persisted in their attempts, and because most were content to accept ease of access to land, sub-division and subsistence. But even where landlords had not resorted to clearances previously, a run of bad seasons and mounting arrears would as in the late 1870s and early 1880s lead to friction.

The condition of many rural dwellers remained bad in these years, and for some may even have worsened. Domestic industry had been an important support to the income of many small occupiers and cottiers or labourers in pre-Famine Ireland. But factory spinning, and at a later date factory weaving, gradually undermined much of this activity: the numbers engaged in textiles falling from 696,000 in 1841 to 218,000 in 1871. By undermining the economy of many small holders, this added to the forces compelling them to throw up their holdings and to drift to the towns or to emigrate. The lot of the farm-labourer was little alleviated in this period. Farmers were increasingly reluctant to grant garden plots to cottiers, and the

Opening of the Dublin and Kingstown Railway, 1834

rural labourer, reduced in status from cottiers, was much more dependent on an exclusively money wage. In the 1860s *The Irish People*, organ of the Fenian movement, complained that 'cruel landlords and ambitious tenants have blotted out every trace of our once numerous cottiers'. While the money wages of the labourer, which had still been as low as 6d a day in the 1840s, had risen to 6s to 9s a week by 1870, the prices of many of his purchases had risen fairly considerably in the same period. Moreover, few labourers could count on regular employment throughout the year, and intermittent unemployment reduced average weekly earnings substantially. Typically the labourer had to seek employment in a variety of locations, and this added to his hardships: 'they sometimes have long distances to travel to and from work, often get wet, and suffer much hardship, not infrequently ending in sickness, disease, and want'. The labourers continued to live in wretched hovels. Unrest among them was widespread in the 1860s, a factor accounting for the participation of many rural labourers in the Fenians.

For many of the towns decay was halted by a widening of their hinterland, as the railways added to their importance as distributing and collecting centres. The main lines from Dublin to Cork, Belfast and Galway were completed between 1851

Belfast water-cart

and 1855. In the following years many secondary lines were constructed, and towns at focal points on the railway network gained in importance at the expense of other towns.

A sharp fall in urban population was evident only in Connaught and in parts of Munster. The fall partly represented the disappearance of the indigent elements which before and during the Famine had crowded into them from poor and overpopulated hinterlands. The relative importance of the towns increased rapidly in post-Famine Ireland from about one-eighth of the population in 1841 to about one-third in 1911. Dublin grew steadily in the second half of the century, the railways enhancing its commercial importance in export and import trade. Belfast continued to grow with remarkable rapidity. With the exception of Derry and a few towns around Belfast, few towns expanded and in consequence they preserved into the twentieth century much of their late eighteenth- and early nineteenth-century character.

Among the social changes flowing from the Famine was an improvement in rural housing, the proportion of houses in the first and second of the Census housing categories rising, and in the third and fourth categories falling. But as late as 1871 there was still a substantial number of houses in the fourth and lowest category—consisting of one-room cabins. Such cabins were still common in the more remote areas, and in the rest of the country were most often the dwellings of farm-labourers. The number of mud-cabins had, however, declined. Of the fourth class of house in 1871, 117,564 were of brick or stone, and 39,177 of mud.

In the growing towns of Dublin and Belfast housing conditions had tended, however, to worsen in the middle decades of the century. In Dublin spacious houses of the Georgian period were beginning to be turned into tenements. In the towns

generally few houses had a water supply, insanitary privies were common, and a single privy might be shared by a number of houses or by all the inhabitants of a tenement-house. Bad water supplies and inadequate drainage in conjunction with overcrowding led to epidemics of diseases such as cholera and typhus. Though they had been slow to get under way, municipal works of drainage and water supply undertaken in the second half of the century made it possible in the long run to reduce the toll of death. In Belfast the rapid expansion of industrial housing greatly reduced the overcrowding which had been evident at an earlier stage of the century. In 1852 7,000 of the city's 10,000 houses were supplied with water only from some 24 fountains, from pumps and from water-carts. By the end of the century, however, the city's municipal water supply was well organized, and the water-closet had almost completely replaced the privy. Similar works had been undertaken in other towns and cities, but in some of the larger towns there was no easing in the overcrowding which was already appalling in the middle of the century. Whole families occupied a single room, and in the crowded tenement-houses of Dublin and of some of the other large towns, Limerick in particular, inadequate sanitation and water supply added to the horrors of overcrowding.

In the towns, even in industrial Belfast, many of the workers were unskilled. The rise in the number of general labourers was striking: from 31,000 in 1841 to 144,000 in 1881. Typically employment was precarious and badly paid. Given uncertain incomes and crowded living conditions, it is hardly surprising that vice flourished in the larger towns. The Census of 1861 returned 147 brothel-keepers and 1,057 prostitutes. These figures—in all probability an underestimate—reflect in particular the circumstances of Dublin, where appalling living conditions and a large military garrison both nourished vice.

In the 1850s and 1860s the rural areas on the whole did well, although the improved fortunes of tenants were in part offset by the low condition of the agricultural labourer and by the general poverty which marked much of the west of the country. In the towns on the other hand, unskilled workers did not at

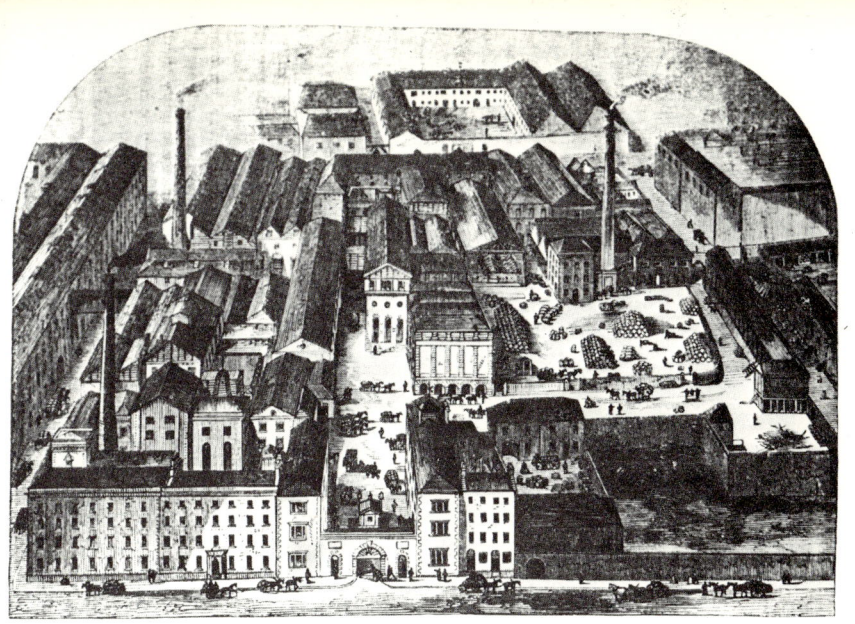

James's Gate Brewery, 1867

all fare well in a period of rising prices. Conditions of employment were also often unhealthy or rigorous, and hours worked were invariably long. Dissatisfaction with conditions was at times reflected in strikes such as the strikes of bakers in many towns against night-work in the late 1850s. While the Fenian movement in the 1860s was political, much of the support for it came from the large pool of social discontent found in the countryside amongst agricultural labourers and small tenants, and in the towns amongst artisans, shop-assistants, and the struggling smaller shopkeepers catering for the modest needs and scant incomes of the poorer classes. The spread of literacy helped to make this discontent articulate. The Fenians were looked on askance by the middle class and by the more substantial tenants.

Nevertheless, the 1850s and 1860s were on balance prosperous, and certainly so by comparison with the difficult conditions emerging in the 1870s. Signs of difficulty in small industrial firms in Dublin and in other towns were appearing before this time. But depression in Britain in the second half of the 1870s enlarged the problem which in Ireland was already beginning to become serious even before general trade recession. Many firms succumbed. The situation also proved serious in rural Ireland, which experienced its first general crisis since the Famine. Prices of agricultural products tumbled at the end of the decade. Competition from new sources of supply was responsible, and a run of bad domestic harvests made the situation all the more serious for the Irish producers. As prices fell sharply while the volume of Irish agricultural output stagnated in the late 1870s and early 1880s, rural incomes declined sharply.

The year 1879 was especially critical because of a disastrously bad harvest. Moreover, with increased foreign supplies, farmers had not even the consolation of rising prices for their diminished output. The price of potatoes alone among agricultural products rose. This had especially serious consequences for the west of Ireland, where a potato diet was still prevalent in the poorer regions. One of the worst hit counties was Mayo. Eighty-five per cent of the holdings in Mayo were below 30 acres. Moreover, because of the large extent of bad land, the valuation of these holdings was far below that of holdings of the same size in other counties—an average of £4 as against £10 in Cork, £12 in Down and £23 in Dublin. All but 12 per cent of the population of the county lived on agricultural holdings, and subsidiary sources of income were very few. It is not surprising that the initiative to found an organization of tenants was taken by a Mayoman, Michael Davitt, and that the first public meeting for this purpose was held in Mayo.

The Land League was intended originally to deal with the problems of high rents and of evictions. But the agitation was political as well, and it derived much of its strength from the support of the Fenians and the political consciousness they had created. Hostility to the landlords, as much political as economic, had been growing before the economic difficulties of the 1870s developed. As early as 1868 Steuart Trench, a perceptive land agent, had noted that 'some look upon the wealthy Saxon and prosperous Protestant as an intruder and interloper who, notwithstanding the prescription of three hundred years, ought now to be deprived of his possessions and expelled from the soil of Ireland'. Unrest over rents was such that in 1881 provision was made for the settlement of rents in land courts. The

Eviction scene, Vandaleur estate, co. Clare

judicial settlement of rents, necessarily downwards in the social and economic conditions of the time, greatly reduced the landlord's legal control of the land which he owned. In a sense a form of dual ownership was created. But this could please neither the landlord whose functions it restricted nor the tenants among whom a demand for unfettered ownership of the land was growing. In such circumstances the policy of buying out the landowners and making the tenants owners, subject to the payment of an annuity to the State, was launched in 1885, and by 1917 almost two-thirds of the occupiers had become owners.

The late 1870s terminated a period of prosperity for the Irish landlords. Even if judicial rent settlement had not been instituted in 1881, rents would have in any event fallen, although not without a much greater amount of unrest and outrage on the part of tenants, and on the part of the landowners, supported by the police, a much larger number of evictions of insolvent or unwilling tenants. During the 1850s and 1860s these times could not be foreseen. The new landlords who purchased encumbered estates were not indebted, and the older landed families that survived the indebtedness of the 1830s and 1840s were the more solvent families, whose financial position improved still further in a period of rising prices and punctual payment of rents. The railways and quickening travel helped, moreover, to widen the horizons of landed families. With better roads, local social life was enriched as well, and tea-parties and social gatherings, more frequent and informal than in the past, helped to break the monotony of rural life in an agreeable fashion. The country-houses still had many servants, and the stables were full. The Bowens of Bowen's Court in co. Cork, for instance, had eight servants, and in the stables had 16 horses not only for hunting but also for the carriages which carried members of the family to and from Mallow railway station and social gatherings in their neighbourhood. When one of the Bowen children made the entry in 1876 in a diary kept by the children—'Mr Rice, the photographer from Mallow, arrived in the morning, he took several views of the house and of us in groups, and he took Mama and Papa on horseback. Miss Flavelle, Sarah, Lizzie and St. John sat in the wagonette. Henry, Mary, Charlie and I stood on the steps. And last of all he drew one of nearly all the labourers'—neither the children nor the photographer can have realized that they were recording a way of life on the verge of extinction.

The position, economic or social and political, of 'ascendancy' families was an assured one into the 1870s. The life of landed families had its urban and related counterpart in the social life of the garrison towns. Affluence and improved communications made possible a varied social life, frequent visits to Dublin or London and often extensive foreign travel. Affluence and family interests both appeared, moreover, enduring to the point of making the Dublin social season a marriage market, even as late as the early 1880s. The political influence of landed families was undermined only in the 1870s, and before that time the families did not regard themselves, nor did the local tenants or inhabitants regard them, as alien to local life and community interests. But the growth of popular political organization in the 1870s and 1880s greatly weakened their position, and reduced their influence, and rising national consciousness with its strong democratic, cultural and even linguistic overtones created a situation in which they were regarded as, and themselves came to feel, intruders. The old-established social order was breaking up at local level, and land reform meant that even where

Farmhouse and family, Clongorey, co. Kildare

landed families did not emigrate from an environment in which they were increasingly alien, the big house was shorn of its acres as well as its political influence. The new system of local government introduced at the end of the century sealed the changes as far as the local administrative power of such families was concerned. What was in a sense an extension of this pattern of life to the capital city—the social life revolving round the Castle—collapsed in 1922 with the establishment of the Irish Free State.

Severe though depression had been in the late 1870s and early 1880s, it came to an end. A recovery in agricultural prices was in part responsible. Moreover, by a further switch from arable, farmers were able to take advantage of more favourable prices for cattle and butter. Economic factors were the main but not the sole ones responsible for the improvement. The judicial rents were on average some 20 per cent lower than the previous rents. The annuities payable by tenants purchasing their holdings were lower still. All the evidence points to rural improvement after 1887. Bank deposits, for instance, rose in every year after 1887 up to 1900. Total deposits and cash balances of the joint stock banks, which had risen only from £24 million in 1870 to £33 million in 1890 almost doubled between then and 1913. Within rural areas especially evidence of poverty lessened. Beggars, still numerous in 1871, became fewer. Bulfin, describing his tour of Ireland by bicycle in 1903, thought it worth his while to relate his meeting a beggar who told him that 'it is not that the country is poorer than it used to be. Its just that there isn't any feelin' in the people for a beggarman.' Barefooted children were also fewer than 30 years previously.

Trade expanded rapidly. While general shopkeepers declined in many areas, this reflected greater mobility and purchasing power in the countryside. Isolated shops carrying petty stocks declined; larger shops and specialist grocers and drapers increased in number. In the most remote regions, however, shops had been virtually non-existent. There small general shops were the first stage in the growth of retail trade. But by the early twentieth century general shops were often declining in these regions also, largely as at an earlier stage in the more prosperous areas as a consequence of increased mobility and of more frequent visits to market-towns. The decline in rural population was a contributory though not the decisive factor. Moreover, there was a substantial rise in retail trade in relative luxuries, the increase in the number of chemists', confectioners', tobacconists' and stationery shops, suggesting that for many their products had become more accessible. Pedlars, once important, had declined sharply in number, and but for the appearance of Jewish pedlars, who helped to introduce to rural households and small retailers new and cheap gadgets such as fountain-pens, eggbeaters and alarm clocks, would have all but disappeared.

A significant feature of the first decade of the twentieth century as revealed by the census returns is the emergence of the bicycle dealer. The bicycle, enhancing mobility, enriched rural life in a way that can hardly be overestimated. Of the Clonmacnoise pattern in September 1903 Bulfin noted that

Shop and post-office, Nobber, co. Meath

'every kind of bicycle procurable is also in evidence'. Motor cars and lorries had also made their appearance. Yet while motor vans carried goods from some creameries to the towns, their use was still very limited. Private cars were still few; in small towns and rural areas the medical doctor was sometimes the first person to introduce the new vehicle. Railway construction in remote areas also helped to increase the mobility of the population at large. The number of railway journeys per head of the population rose from 2·9 to 6·2 between 1871 and 1900. In the poorer parts of the country people had as a matter of course walked distances of 20–30 miles. But the bicycle or the cheap railway ticket on market-days altered this. It also meant that people had access to shops in the larger market-towns, and may have been the reason for a decline in the number of rural shops in some areas.

The bicycle in rural Ireland

Housing and diet also improved. The number of one-room houses on agricultural holdings was still 16,891 in 1891, but fell to 7,683 in 1901 and 3,872 in 1911. In remote areas outhouses for animals had become more common by the 1890s, and the practice of keeping animals within the living-room at night, once common among the poorer families in such areas, was declining rapidly. Diet improved as well. The fall in the potato acreage from 1,043,583 acres in 1870 to 635,321 in 1900 was much sharper than the fall in population. The year 1901 was the thirteenth successive year of decline in the potato acreage.

Literacy spread rapidly in the course of the second half of the century. The proportion of the population between five and 15 attending school at the time of Census-taking rose from 20 per cent in 1841 to 46·5 per cent in 1881. These figures underestimate the proportion of children who received some schooling because in rural areas especially many children attended intermittently or for a few years only. The rise in the proportion of children aged nine in attendance is more meaningful: it rose from 34 per cent in 1851 to 65 per cent in 1881. In the poorer areas many children had to herd animals on their own land or were sent to work as farm-servants at an age as early as nine. Schooling for them was short-lived, and there were many adults in these areas in the final decades of the century who had in their youth little, if any, experience of school. In his autobiography, Paddy the Cope from Dungloe related that his father had never spent a single day at school. In the parish of Tullaghobegley, the worst in Donegal, 72 per cent of the population aged five and upwards, was returned as illiterate in the 1881 Census. By 1911, however, the proportion of the total child population of nine years in Ireland not in attendance was only 14 per cent, and regularity of attendance had also greatly

Ellison Street, Castlebar

An early motor car in front of the Spa Hotel Restaurant, Lucan

improved, 65 per cent of the children enrolled for the year attending for 100 days or more as against 42 per cent in 1861. Compulsory attendance may have contributed to this result, but its success has to be seen against a background of rising attendance throughout the century.

The effects of literacy were far reaching. As early as 1861 the Census Commissioners, noting that knowledge of reading was more widespread than writing, had attributed it in part to 'the ready access which the present low prices afford to newspapers and other cheap periodicals'. Its results were reflected also in more widespread interest and participation in the popular political movements of the period, and even more strikingly in support for the linguistic and cultural objectives of the Gaelic League, founded in 1893. Bulfin, in 1907, noted of Wexford, that 'there are nearly 40 branches of the Gaelic League, and most of them are in the farming districts'. It contributed as well to the striking success of the Gaelic Athletic Association in rural Ireland.

Even the farm-labourer's lot eased a little. Through emigration their numbers had declined much more sharply than did the number of farmers and relatives assisting on farms. In consequence a shortage of labour was beginning to emerge in rural areas, at any rate during the busy months. This was reflected in wage rates. By the mid-1890s farm-labourers earned about 10*s* a week. In 1907 wages averaged 11*s* 3*d*, and were above 13*s* in the vicinity of Dublin and Belfast. Nevertheless, they were still below urban wages for an unskilled labourer. In the mid-1890s a bricklayer's labourer in Belfast earned 18s. Intermittent employment reduced earnings still further. The labourers were still living in the late nineteenth century in one-room hovels: their families were poorly clothed, their children barefooted. Food itself was often scarce: for some families, except for the wage-earner, even an egg was a luxury, and the children were undernourished, at times even hungry. A social gulf separated the labourer and his family from the small farmer. When the building of labourers' cottages was instituted by the local authorities, farmers, though adequately compensated, were not only reluctant to provide plots of land for their construction, but in some instances could not conceive what a labourer could do with a two-storey house.

Change was also evident in the poor and remote lands along the west coast, hitherto almost untouched by change. In many districts in these areas, population had continued to expand after the Famine, emigration was less extensive than from better-off parts, and as a result poverty remained general: 'in the congested districts there are two classes, namely the poor and the destitute. There are hardly any resident gentry; there are a few traders and officials; but nearly all the inhabitants are either poor or on the verge of poverty—the poor mainly support the destitute.' Housing, diet, clothing, furnishing were all unsatisfactory. Agricultural methods were primitive; the land itself barren.

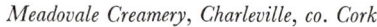
Meadovale Creamery, Charleville, co. Cork

Children outside Carbury National School, co. Kildare

Rents were not the problem in these areas. Except for the very poor families with cash incomes of as little as £10 per annum, rents of £1 or £2 for a holding could hardly be regarded as oppressive. The real problem was that farms were too small to afford an adequate living to a family, even if rent had not to be taken into account. In the better-off areas or families, cash incomes of around £40 or £50 depended largely on earnings gained outside local agriculture. For instance, a high proportion of families in some areas depended on money earned by migratory workers who went seasonally to Scotland or to farms in more prosperous parts of the country. In Donegal circumstances frequently forced families to send children of eight or nine as farm-servants in the 'Lagan' or eastern part of the county. In 1883 Paddy the Cope was, as he related in his autobiography, sent at the age of ten to the 'Lagan' because 'the year before had been a bad year in Scotland, and my father had not enough money home with him to pay the rent and the shop debts'. Another Donegal man who has left us an account of his life, Micky MacGowan, walked in 1874 at the age of nine the 30 miles from his home in north-west Donegal, accompanied by his mother, to the hiring fair at Letterkenny. Five or six seasons spent in this fashion on farms in eastern Donegal was generally a prelude to migratory work in Scotland.

In bad years such as the early 1880s the labourer might take home as little as £2 10s after a season in Scotland but in better years net earnings might amount to £8 or £10.

While sprigging or embroidery work was declining, shirt-making in the Inishowen Peninsula and knitting in Glenties and outlying areas, made it possible for the womenfolk to add to the family income. In these areas migratory labour was comparatively unimportant; in other areas from 20 to 50 per cent of the labour force departed seasonally. Shirtmaking and knitting were poorly remunerated: the average weekly family income from knitting in the Rosses in the early 1890s was 4s. But low though these earnings were or the sums migratory workers brought home with them, it was precisely this income which prevented poverty from being worse, and the families or areas which had recourse to neither source of income were the poorest of all.

Appalling though the condition of the west and north was in the late 1870s and the early 1880s, some of the misery was quite unusual even for these areas and was the combined result of general price decline and poor potato crops. As a result family indebtedness to rural traders mounted, and could be substantially reduced only as prices improved. Indeed, but for the presence of the rural trader and his readiness to extend credit, the plight of the people would have been even more desperate. In this way the gradual though limited growth of trade in these areas in preceding decades may have prevented deaths from starvation in a manner which had not in the past been confined to the period of the Great Famine. The real weakness of the situation was that, where competition was limited, price and crop failure put the trader in a position to place an excessive value on the undoubted very real service he rendered to the small holder. In particular in areas where markets for agricultural produce were limited, the small farmer had to sell his produce to the same trader who supplied him with his purchases. The absence of competition made it possible for the trader to reduce the rates he paid for the agricultural produce and to inflate the value of the goods he supplied. The fact that in parts of Donegal as, for instance, in the large Dunfanaghy Poor Law

Union, the number of traders actually declined in the difficult conditions of the 1870s, strengthened the hand of those who survived.

In areas where trade did not contract, however, the same condition of monopoly did not apply. In the Clifden Union the number of shops rose in the 1870s and later in the early 1890s a Congested Districts Board inspector reported 'a large number of country shops scattered through these districts'. In areas close

Spriggers at work, Ardara, co. Donegal

to markets, and especially in the south-west, the small holders in the congested districts sold their produce for cash to produce dealers or on the markets, and for this reason local shopkeepers, even though they provided goods on credit to local farmers, were not in the monopoly position which enabled them to exact the usurious charges which they succeeded in doing among the small holders of parts of the north-west. In Donegal, even the knitting work passed through the hands of the traders, who paid the knitters in kind, forcing them to take commodities such as tea even if they did not want them. Moreover, 'although the price paid for socks is nominally 1s 6d yet since this is generally

(*overleaf*) *The port of Dublin in the 1880s*

taken in tea and always in goods, 1s 2d is about the actual money value'.

By the early 1890s the worst was over in the congested districts along the west coast. Debts had not increased in recent years; in many cases they had been reduced. The traders themselves had frequently been anxious to have their customers reduce their indebtedness, as the accounts run up in bad years took two to three years to clear off, and for the trader 'two bad seasons in succession would be disastrous as the shopkeeper's resources are limited'. Cash dealings were beginning to replace credit dealings. In Glenties itself, moreover, the main firm distributing yarn to the knitters had always as a matter of principle paid for knitting in cash. While in very backward districts such as Gweedore credit dealings still predominated in the early 1890s, they were declining elsewhere. In the Rosses purchases for cash were as numerous as on credit. In Glenties competition had already significantly reduced the prices of goods supplied on credit. The extra charge for a 13s bag of meal supplied on credit, once 5s or 7s 6d, had been reduced to 2s.

Improvement in the congested districts was general in the 1890s and in the first decade of the twentieth century. Recovery in prices, higher earnings by migrant workers in Scotland, better transport facilities and greater emigration were the principal factors accounting for the improvement. It was against this background that the efforts undertaken by the Congested Districts Board established in the 1890s to improve husbandry and fishing, transfer holdings to the tenants and establish local industries, began to take effect. The congested districts were the last areas in which an older and more easy-going way of life survived. Of funerals in the Spiddal area in co. Galway, a Congested Districts Board inspector had noted that 'they often cause expense which the bereaved families can ill sustain, as well as the loss of valuable time to whole villages in which a death has occurred and throughout which, as a mark of respect to the deceased, all work, even of the most important kind, must remain in abeyance until after the funeral'. These districts were also the last in which Irish remained the spoken language. But even within them greater contact with the outside world was bringing about changes. A striking indication of this is the decline in the numbers speaking Irish only. Their numbers declined sharply from 64,167 in 1881 to 16,873 in 1911.

The population of Belfast rose from 100,000 in 1851 to 387,000 in 1911; that of Dublin, including suburbs, from 321,000 to 398,000. The population of the other towns as a whole declined by some 12 per cent in this period. Moreover, in larger and smaller towns alike, economic activity depended mainly on distribution. Apart from industries processing agricultural raw materials, such as brewing, malting, milling and distilling, industry had tended to contract, so that even where the growth of trade and the advent of the railways had increased employment, a disproportionately large part of the employment consisted of unskilled work, badly paid and casual. This was true not only of provincial towns but also of Dublin, where the numbers employed in industry were small in relation to the total labour force.

A Dublin carter, New Row

The earnings of 1,254 Dublin families covered by an enquiry in 1910 averaged 22s 2d a week. The earnings of individual families ranged from under 5s to over 60s, but the larger proportion received less than 20s per week. The average earnings of family heads were 15s 11½d; other income (principally earnings of other members of the family) averaged 6s 2½d. In Dublin, for many families earnings were at best barely adequate to cover food and rent, leaving nothing for other necessities such

Workers leaving shipbuilding yards, Queen's Island, Belfast

as clothing and medical care. Moreover, the casual nature of the employment of many meant that at any time as much of the labour force as one-fifth was out of work, making their plight all the more desperate. Skilled workers fared much better. Significantly, too, it was among skilled workers with less fear of unemployment that trade unions had made some headway. In the 1890s more than a half of the country's 40,000 to 50,000 trade unionists were to be found in the north. In Belfast at the outset of the twentieth century some 9,000 were employed in the shipbuilding yards of Harland and Wolff; many were also employed in the yards of a second firm, and in the engineering industry. Belfast itself had much unskilled labour as well. But even for the families of the unskilled, prospects were brighter there than elsewhere because of female employment in the city's huge linen industry. The linen industry employed twice or three times as many female workers as males. While the average earnings of operatives in the linen industry at 12s 6d in 1910 were said to be low because of the readiness with which women accepted low-wage employment, such earnings nevertheless supplemented the earnings of the family in a substantial way in comparison with the meagre average figures not simply for female but for all other family earnings of 6s 2½d in Dublin in the same year. With prices rising in the early twentieth century, the position of many workers tended to deteriorate. Prior to the 1908 strike the dockers in Cork had not had a wage increase in 20 years. Rising unrest was testified to in strikes in Belfast, Cork, Wexford, culminating in the great lock-out in Dublin in 1913, made all the more bitter because the issues revolved not simply round wages or conditions, but round union recognition by the employers. The position of the mass of the unskilled labourers was made worse in Dublin by appalling housing conditions, unequalled in the rising industrial towns in Britain and worse even than conditions in Glasgow and Liverpool. Bad housing conditions were not confined to Dublin—to a greater or lesser extent they were to be found in most large towns, Limerick especially. In Dublin in 1914 nearly 26,000 families lived in 5,000 tenement-houses. Of these some 20,000 had only a single room, and another 5,000 had two rooms. In all, some 87,000 people lived in these conditions. Many of the tenement-houses were in a bad state of preservation: 1,500 were estimated to be incapable of being made fit for habitation. As late as 1926, according to the Census of that year, 27·8 per cent of the city's population lived in single-room tenements; 23·4 per cent of its population were living four or more to a room. Cork and Limerick had a high proportion of their population living in similar conditions. Conditions in most other towns were in no way as appalling. In Belfast in particular, despite its rapid growth, there had been much building, and by the appalling standards elsewhere, its housing was comparatively good. The effects of improved sanitation and water supply were slow enough in taking place. In the late nineteenth century, the urban death-rate was higher than the rural, and epidemic disease was still common. In Dublin with its crowded tenements of underpaid families, conditions conducive to ill-health were particularly prevalent. In nearly every tenement, according to contemporary evidence, 'human excreta is to be found ... scattered about the yard ... and in some cases even in the passages of the house itself'. The death-rate in Dublin in 1901–10 was significantly higher than in Belfast. Child mortality was also very high.

As the centres of large towns were invaded by commerce or by the poor, an exodus of the well-to-do to new residential districts in the suburbs began. This exodus was especially striking in Dublin, and as the century progressed the contrast sharpened between the festering poverty of the overcrowded and extending tenement districts and the new suburban areas. The continued development of the latter would have been impossible without the advent of suburban railways, horse-drawn buses and from the 1870s trams, first horse-drawn and then electrified. Moreover, the more prosperous families could escape the towns for holidays at the seaside, and seaside towns and hotels expanded. Dublin, in particular, because of its commercial and administrative importance, had a large middle class, which continued to grow. Moreover, on top of its lawyers, doctors, merchants and shop-keepers, nineteenth-century business and administration gave rise to a growing amount of clerical employment. Government offices, large banking concerns, transport companies and great industrial firms such as Guinness each employed its own army of clerks, and wholesalers, importers and other firms, though individually employing few, collectively provided a large amount of clerical employment. Not all clerks enjoyed the relatively favourable remuneration of civil servants and bank clerks. Nevertheless, many clerical workers were in a position to flee the decaying central districts, and to provide better housing for themselves and education for their families. Among better-paid families holidays at the seaside were a matter of course. The rise in clerical employment was impressive in the late nineteenth century. Excluding civil servants and bank and railway clerks, the number of male commercial clerks almost doubled between 1871 and 1911. Striking also at the end of the period, and coinciding with, although not necessarily a result of, the advent of the typewriter, was the sharp rise in the number of female commercial clerks, their number more than doubling from 3,437 in 1901 to 7,849 in 1911.

At the centre of Dublin social life at its highest level stood the Viceroy. The sharpest distinction was that between those on the Viceregal invitation list, and those not on it. Landed, professional and army families predominated in this life. This meant that successful families in business or commerce strove to identify themselves with their way of life and even with the districts where they dwelt. Temple Road in the 1880s was described by Louie Bennett as 'the refuge of highly respectable business people anxious to escape from the social zone allotted to the world of trade and commerce'. In such a district 'social contacts were few and cautious. The wholesale merchant, was on a different footing from the retailer. Grocer or auctioneer was ill-at-ease on Temple Road, but biscuits and furniture held high place. And tea won distinction through the society of Friends. . . . In the '80s the Catholics were still struggling to penetrate professional circles and were not accepted without question within the fold of Temple Road.' This pattern of social life and the attitudes that went with it survived until English rule collapsed in 1921. With the departure of the Viceroy and his immediate circle, its centre fell apart. Its break-up was thus in part a result of political revolution, but not wholly. The wane of the landed classes, the rise of national consciousness with its racial, cultural and historic outlook, and the inevitable impact on social life of modern democratic aspirations would have brought about the change in any event. Some attempt was made to re-create a social life with some similarities to the old around the office of Governor-General, but it succumbed to the spirit of a new and different age.

Dublin slum, Poole Street

Setting aside social distinctions within the middle and upper classes, the poverty and overcrowding of the poorer quarters and the ease and comfort denoted by the new residential districts afforded a growing contrast. The contrast and the growing remoteness between the two aspects of urban life was not specifically Irish, but in most Irish towns the contrast was sharpened by the absence of industrialization and by the consequent growth of a large mass of unrelieved poverty and hopelessness. In rural Ireland the main physical change was occasioned by emigration. A declining population was in itself a big change, but it served also to limit changes in some respects by reducing the pressures intensifying land use and by slowing the process of renewing or expanding structures in villages and in the rural landscape. Apart from the political revolution and its immediate social impact conditions changed only slowly in the twentieth century in Ireland, in some respects very little before the 1950s. Moreover, given a declining population and limited industrialization, the vestiges of expansion in village, town and countryside in the second half of the eighteenth century and early nineteenth century have often been remarkably well preserved.

Further Reading

E. Bowen, *Bowen's Court*, 1942
M. Carbery, *The farm by Lough Gur*, 1937
J. Carty, *Ireland from the Great Famine to the Treaty, 1851–1921*, 1951
J. Connolly, *Labour in Irish history*, 1910
W. P. Coyne (ed.), *Ireland, industrial and agricultural*, 1902
P. Gallagher, *My story. By Paddy the Cope*, 1939
J. H. Harvey, *Dublin: a study in environment*, 1949
E. Jones, *A social geography of Belfast*, 1960
E. Larkin, *James Larkin: Irish Labour leader, 1876–1947*, 1965
P. Lynch and J. Vaizey, *Guinness's brewery in the Irish economy, 1759–1876*, 1960
M. Mac Gabhann, *Rotha mór an tsaoil*, 1959 (English translation, *The hard road to Klondike*, 1962)
E. Strauss, *Irish nationalism and British democracy*, 1951
W. Steuart Trench, *Realities of Irish life*, 1966
L. M. Cullen, *An economic history of Ireland since 1660*, 1972
J. S. Donnelly, jnr., *The land and the people of nineteenth-century Cork*, 1975
J. J. Lee, *The modernisation of Irish society*, 1973
B. L. Solow, *The land question and the Irish economy 1870–1903*, 1971

Index

Entries in **bold** type denote pages with illustrations.

Abbacies, 11
Abercorn, Earl of, 79
Agriculture, 2–4, 8, 15–16, 17, 27, 31, **32**, 33–5, **51**, 52, **79**, 80, **81**, 82–3, 144–5, 152–3, 155, 162
Ale, 16, 17, 45
Ale-houses, 68
Altamont, Lord, 119
Andrews, 109
Annals of Innisfallen, 45
Ardara, co. Donegal, **163**
Ardart, co. Kerry, 31
Ardglass, **95**
Armagh, 22
   Book of, 22
   co., 82, 107
Arthur, Dr Thomas, 62
Assemblies, 17
   see also Fairs
Athenry, 23, 66
Athy, 78
Axe, **25**
Ailenn, 9

Balle, Thomas, 35
Ballinasloe, 72, 74
Ballynahinch, co. Galway, 132
Balybothy, co. Tipperary, 33
Banagher, 72
Banking, 73
Bantry, 134, 140
Barrow, river, 23, 78
Beggars, 116, 126, 136, 155–6
Belcher, William, **136**
Belfast, **90**, **105**, 125, 132, 134, 137, **138**, 144, 147, **148**, 150, 159–60, 167, **168**, 169
Belmullet, co. Mayo, 132
Bennett, Louie, 170
Betagh, 32–4
Bianconi, **133**
Bicycle, 156, **157**
Black Death, 34, 37
Black Pig's Dyke, 5
Blackrock, co. Louth, 133
Book of Armagh, 22
   composed at Kildare, **21**
   of Lismore, 48

Borde, Andrew, 27, 35, 43, 45
Boru, Brian, 22
Bowen, 154
Bowen's Court, 154
Boyne, river, 1, 2, 3
Brady, Hugh, bishop of Meath, 46
Brehon laws, 26
Breitheamh, 12
Brereton, 66
Bridges, 54
Bristol, 43
Brittany, 1, 4
Bronze Age, 2, 4, 14
Bulfin, William, 155, 156–7
Bundoran, 5
Bush, J., 79, 91
Byerley, Thomas, 79

Cahir, 5
Cahirciveen, 132
Caldwell, Sir James, 103
Caledon, co. Tyrone, 103
Callan, co. Kilkenny, 139
Campion, Edmund, 41
Canals, **78**, 79, 132
   Grand Canal, 78, 132
   Newry Canal, 78
   Royal Canal, 132
Carbery, co. Cork, 77
Carbury, co. Kildare, **161**
Carlow, 24
Carolan, Turlough, 102, 105
Carr, Sir John, 78
Carriages, 68, 75
   see also Coaches and coaching
Carrick [-on-Suir], 56, 81
Carrickfergus, 112
Cartage, **75**, 77–8, **167**
Carton, 104
Cashel, 5
Cashel, archdiocese of, 95
Casse, Steven, 40
Castide, Henry, 27, 29, 42, 43, 47
Castlebar, **158**
Castlecomer, 86, 112
   Lord, 112
Castlehaven, co. Cork, 98
Castlemartyr, co. Cork, 62
Castles, 23, 30–1, 56

173

INDEX

Catholic, Catholics, 93–4, **95**, 96–8, 101, 126–7, 137, 171
Cattle Acts, 51
Cattle-raids, 14–15, 18, **30**, 31
Cavan, 29
Céilí, 11–12, 16
Celtic race, 4
Census, 99–100, 134, 138, 150, 156, 157–9
Charleville, co. Cork, **160**
Chieftains, Irish, 23–4, **28**, 29, 30, **44, 46, 47**
Christ Church Cathedral, manor at Clonkeen, 31, 34
Christianity, 10–11, 13–14, 21
Church of Ireland, 95, 126
Clare, co., 22, 59, 78, 100
Clarendon, 56
Clayton, Mrs, 104
Clifden, 129, 132
  Poor Law Union, 163
Clongorey, co. Kildare, **155**
Clonmacnoise, 6, **10**
Clonmel, 109, 133
Coaches and coaching, **68**, 75–6, 132–3
  see also Stage-coaches
Coffee-houses, 68
Coinage, 9, 21
Collon, co. Louth, 80
Comber, co. Down, 108, 109, 112
Common Law, English, 25, 26
Commons, House of, 93, 101
Concubinage, 7, 41
Congested Districts, 160–7
  Board, 163, 166
Connaught, 23, 81, 82, 110, 116, 121, 122, 125, 128, 139, 148
Connemara, 77, 128, 129, 132
Conolly, Mrs, Castletown, 103
Cork, 30, **67, 73**, 74, 76, 78, 87, **88**, 123, **129**, 134, 137, 139, 147, 168, 169
  co., 50, 70, 77, 81, 98, 122, 128, 152, 154
Costeret, Bryan, 43
Cottiers, 34, 110–15, **116**, 117, 119–21, 123, 144, 146–7
Coulthurst, Sir John, 77
Court of Exchequer, **23**
Crafts, 9, 13
  see also Occupations
Crannógs, 6
Creaghting, 50
Creton, 25, 29, 45
Cruachain, 9
Curragh, co. Kildare, 62

Dancing, **64**, 115, **142**
Davitt, Michael, 152
Defenders, 127
Delany, Mrs, 102, 103
  see also Mrs Pendarves
Delany family, 105
Derbhfine, 11
Derry, **54, 86**, 132, 139, 144, 148
  co., 101
  diocese of, 96
Devon Commission, 120
Diet, 2, 3, 4, 15–16, 60, 118, 122–3, 152, 157, 160
Disease, 13, 37, 110, 169
Dissenters, 95
Donegal, co., 5, 72, 77, 81, 103, 124, 128, 129, 158, 161, 162, 163
Down, co., 5, 82, 112, 152
Dress, 47–8
Drogheda, 54, 55, 66
Druid, 12
Dobbs, Arthur, 90
Dublin, 20, 23, 24, 28, 35, 36, 37, **38**, 39, 48, 52, 53, 55, 64, 65–7, **68**, 70, 73, 74, 75, 76, 78, 79, 81, 83, **87**, 88, **89**, 90, **91**, 95, 101, 110, 116, 123, 132, 135–7, 140, 144, 147, 148, 150, 151, 154, **164–5**, **167**, 169, 170, **171**
  archdiocese of, 95
  co., 32, 61, 152
  Society, 104
  Zoological Gardens, **135**
Dunboyne, co. Meath, 46
Dundalk, 57, 85
Dunfanaghy Poor Law Union, co. Donegal, 162–3
Dungannon, 129
Dungloe, co. Donegal, 158
Dunloe, co. Kerry, 84
Dunton, 53, 55, 60–1, 62, 64, 65, 66

Eamhain Macha, 9
Edgeworth, Richard Lovell, 99, **103**
  Maria, **103**
Elizabeth I, 68
Emancipation, Catholic, 137, 139
Emigration, **129**, 144, 166, 171
Enclosure, 8, 35, 84
Engels, Frederick, 136
English language, 26, 28
Enniskillen, 132
Erris, co. Mayo, 77
Estate management, 71, 84, 103–4
Evictions, **153**
Eyre, Stratford, 76

174

INDEX

Factions, faction-fights, 108–9, 126
Fairs, 18, 22, 30, 72, 109
  of Carman, 22
  see also Assemblies
Famine, 45, 82–4, 118
  Great, 142, 144, 145, 152, 160, 162
Farmers, 110–11, 119, 120, **127**, 128, **155**
Felicia, daughter of John, 44
Fenians, 147, 151
Fermanagh, co., 81
Fermoy, 76
Ferry, **54**
Field system, 3, 8
  see also Enclosure
File, 12
Fingal, near Dublin, 65
Fires and fire-fighting, 6, **7**, **85**
Firmarii, 32–3
Fishing, 2, **37**, 38
Flaith, flatha, 11–12
Folk-tales, 18
Football, 65
Fords, 9, 54
Forests, 1–2, 3, 5, 50, 58–9, 68, 86
Forster, Robert, 73
Forth, barony of, co. Wexford, 56
Foster, Sir John, 80
Fosterage, 7
Foyle, river, **54**, 73
France, 41
French language, 26
Froissart, 27
Funerals, 64, 166

Gaelic Athletic Association, 159
Gaelic League, 159
Galbraith, Hugh, 73
Gallowglasses (*Gallóglaigh*), 25
Galway, 23, 35, 36, 37–8, 44, 47, **65**, 66, 76, 85, 110, 129, 147
  co., 99, 108, 112, **125**, 138, 166
Gamble, John, 91
Gandon, 104
Gavillers, 32
Gentlemen, **94**
Giant's Causeway, 133
Giraldus Cambrensis, 22, 25, 27, 31, 40, 41, 43
Glandore, co. Cork, 98
Glendalough, 6, 133
Glenties, co. Donegal, 162, 166
Gloucester, Earl of, **29**
Gookin, Vincent, 52, 61
Gorey, 111
Gowran, co. Kilkenny, 76

Grain, 2, 3, 4, 15–16, 31, 45, 51, 52, 74, 118
Grand Canal, **78**, 135
Grange Ring-fort, **7**
Greene, Thomas, 70
Guilds, 35, 38–40
  Tailors' Guild, 35, 39–40
  Weavers' Guild, 39
Guinness brewery, **151**, 170
Gweedore, co. Donegal, 166

Handel's *Messiah*, 106
Harland and Wolff, Belfast, 168
Harpers, **17**, 18
  Harp Festival, **105**
Harvests, 16, 45, 51, 83, 84, 114, 118, 122, 152
Henry VIII, 47
Horses, **8**, **9**, **54**, **101**
  Horse-races, 62, 108, 109
  see also Races
Hospitals, 110, 140
Hotels, **78**, 79, **159**, 170
Housing, 6, **7**, 20–1, **53**, **55**, **61**, 62, **66**, 68, 106–7, 115, **116**, 123, 148–9, **155**, 157, 160, 169, **171**
Huguenots, 67
Hunting, 2, 3, 4, 18, **33**, **71**
Hurling, 44, 65, **109**

Iar-Connacht, 60
Iberia, 1, 4
Illiteracy, *see* Literacy
Inauguration of an Irish chieftain, **28**
Inchiquin, Lady, 62
Industry, 86, **87**, **88**, 145, 167–8
  domestic, 146–7
Inglis, H. D., 128
Inishowen, 162
Innisfallen, *see* Annals of
Inns, 10, **54**, 55, 79, **132**, 133
Irish Free State, 155
Irish language, 26, 28, 138–40, 166–7
Iron Age, 5, 14
  -working, 4, 9, 50, 86
Iveragh, co. Kerry, 77, 132

James II, 86
James's Gate Brewery, **151**

Kells, **134**
Kenmare, 140
  Earl of, 85
  estate, 84
  Fourth Viscount, 94
Kerry, co., 70, 77, 78, 97, 98, 99, 100, 120, 122, 124, 128, 129, 132

175

INDEX

Kilbaha beach, **139**
Kilcock, 87
Kildare, 66, 155
  book composed at, **21**
  co., 52, 57, 60, 64
  Ninth Earl of, 48
Kilkenny, 24, **56**, 73, 75, 79, 142
  co., 98, 139
Killarney, 75, 85, 116, 133
Kilruddery, co. Wicklow, **71**
Kings, Irish, **24**
Knights in armour, **22**
Knitting, 162–3
Knockaulin, 9
Kohl, J. G., 140

La Gras, Sibilla, 31
Labourers, 34, **122**, 146–7, 150, 159–60, 167–8
Land, changes in ownership of, 57, 58, 71, 93–4, 153, 155
  League, 152
  purchase, 153
  reform, 154
Landed classes, position of, 93
  social life of, 153–4
  wane of, 171
Lanesborough, Viscount, 56
Languages spoken in Ireland, 26, 28
De Latocnaye, 86, 87, 91, 98, 104, 109, 113, 116
Law tracts, early Irish, 6, 7, 8, 11, 14, 16, 17
Leenane, co. Galway, 132
Le Foulere, John, 44
Leighlinbridge, 78
Leinster, 23, 24, 81, 122, 124, 127
  Duke of, 104
  King of, 20
Letterkenny, 161
Lewis, Samuel, 133
Lifford, 103, 108
Limerick, 30, 75, **77**, 78, 85, 91, 100, 134, 150, 169
  co., 119, 122, 128
Linen, 72, 81, **82**, **83**, 93, 107–8, **113**, **136**, **138**, 168
Lisburn, 53
Lismore, Book of, 48
Listowel, 112
Literacy, 99–100, 102–3, 112, 138, 157–9
Lock-out, 168
London, 66, 91, 135, 154
Lough, Corrib, 78
Lough Neagh, 78

Loughrea, 83
Louth, co., 80, 133
Lucan, **159**
Luckombe, Philip, 88
Lurgan, 82

MacCarthy Reagh, Finghin, 48
Mac Conmara, Donnchadh Ruadh, 98
MacGowan, Micky, 161
MacHale, Archbishop, 139
MacMorrogh, Art, **29**
MacMurchadha, Donnchadh, 24
Mails, 76
Malahide, 35
Mallow, 75, 154
Marches, 26
Martin, 132
Massareene, Lord, 59
Maynooth, 132, 137
Mayo, co., 77, 99, 128, 140, 152
Meadovale Creamery, Charleville, co. Cork, **160**
Meath, co., 9, 13, 107, 119, 134, **156**
Medicine and medical men, 13, 40–1, 62, 96, 140
Megaliths, 2–3, 5
Menlough, co. Galway, 124
Merriman, Brian, 100
Mesolithic Age, 1
Metal working, 2
Middle class, 151, 170
Middlemen, 101–2, 111
Migrant, migratory, labour, 100, 112 114–15, 121–2, 161–2, 166
Mills, 16, 17, **52**, **53**
Monaghan, **61**
  co., 120, 146
Monasteries, **10**, **11**, 15–16, 18, 20, 26
Monks, **15**, **35**
De Montbret, Coquebert, 85, 99, 109
Montpellier, 41
Moriz, Sir John, **27**
Morris, Dr, 62
Motor car, 157, **159**
Motte and bailey, 23
Muckross, co. Kerry, 78
Mulholland's linen mill, Belfast, **136**
Mullingar, 53, 72
Munster, 124, 126, 128, 148
Music, 18, 40, 43–4, 64, 105–6, 115
Mystery plays, 40

Navigation, 1
Nedeen, co, Kerry, 77
Neolithic Age, 2

176

INDEX

New Ross, 23, 78
Newgrange, 2
Newry, 5, 78
 Canal, 78
Newspapers, 53, 102
Nicholls, George, 126, 141
Nimmo, Alexander, 129
Nobber, co. Meath, **156**
Nobleman, **57**
Norman-French, 26, 28
Norman invasion, 23
 (Anglo-Irish) Lordship, 23, 24, 25–6, 27–8
 conflict with Irish, 23–5
Norse, 20–3

Oakboys, 126
O'Brien, Colonel Daniel, 59
O'Bruadair, David, 58, 60
Occupations, 38, 81
 see also Crafts
O'Coileáin, Seán, 97–8
O'Connell, Daniel, 137, 139
O'Domhnaill, Seán Clárach, 70
O'Donnell, Manus, 29
O'Donovan, John, 132
O'Flaghertie, 60, 61
O'Hagan, **27**
O'Hanlon, Redmond, 57
Omagh, **55**, 110, 129
O'Moghane, Donal, 44
O'Murchadha, Seán na Raithíneach, 98
O'Neill, **28**
 Turloch, **47**
O'Rahilly, Egan, 70
Orange Order, 127
Ormonde, First Countess of, **40**
 Tenth Earl of, 56
 Duke of, **56**
Orrerys, 103
Osbertstown, 78
O'Súilleabháin, Amhlaoibh, 139
 Eoghan Ruadh, 99, 100, 112, 114–15
Oxford, 48
O'Sullivan, Dennis, 98

Paddy the Cope, 158, 161
Palaeolithic Age, 1
Pale, 24, 35, 47
Parliament, parliamentary, 24, 30, 44, 75, 79, 91, 96, 100, 101, 104
Peasant, **120, 123**
Peasantry, **114**
Pedlars, 53, 73, 156
Peep O'Day Boys, 126

Pendarves, Mrs, 102, 104, 106
 see also Mrs Delany
Petty, Sir William, 53, 61
Pig drover, **121**
Plague, 37
Planter families, 70
Police, 140
Poor Law, 115, 140–1
Population growth, 3, 15, 18, 50, 84, 118, 119, 120, 134
 decline, 144, 172
Portobello, Dublin, 79
Portumna, co. Galway, 109
Post, 55–6
Postmaster General, 76
Potato diet, 60, 122–3, 142, 152, 157, 162
Presbyterian, 126
Protestant, 101, 127, 152
Public house, **149**
Von Puckler-Muskau, H. L. H., 133

Race-meetings, 101
Races, 142
 see also Horses: Horse-races
Raftery, Anthony, 115, 139
Railways, **147**, 148, 153, 157, 170
Rallahine, co. Clare, **59**
Rapparees, 57
Rath, 5–6
Rathcline House, co. Longford, 56–7
Rawdon, Sir George, 53
Rebellion of 1798, 127, 129
Reformation, 58
Renaissance, 48
Rents, 72, 111–12, 119, 120, 152–3, 155, 161, 167
Revolution, Industial, 62
Ribbonmen, 127
Richard II, 25, 29, **43**, 45
Ring-fort, 5–6, **7**, 9
Roads, 9–10, 54–5, 73–4, **74**, 75–7, 128–9
Robertstown, co. Kildare, 79
De Rocheford, Jorevin 96
Rosponte, 23
Rosses, co. Donegal, 72, 162, 166
Roundstone, co. Galway, 132
Rustic pastime, **108**

St Columbanus, penitential of, 6, 13
St Leger, 29
Sanitation, 35–6, 150, 169
Scandinavia, 1, 20
Schools, 41, 96–7, **98**, 99–101, 138–9, 157–9, **161**

177

INDEX

Scotland, 161–2, 166
Scottish farmers, 132, 145
  gardeners, 102
Scott, Sir Walter, 135
Scribe, **11**
Sea-bathing, 109–10, **111**, 133–4
Sedan-chair, **137**
Shannon, **77**, 78
  Harbour, 79
Ship, **36**
Shirtmaking, 162
Shops, 66, **73**, **145**, **156**, 162–3, 166
Slane, co. Meath, 119
Slaves, slavery, 9, 13–14, 22
Sligo, co., 119
Slums, 90–1, 136–7, 148, 150, 169, **171**
Souterrains, 14
Spiddal, co. Galway, 166
Spinning, 81, 113, 125, 146
Sprigging, 162, **163**
Stage-coaches, 55, 76, **130–1**
  see also Coaches and Coaching
Staplestown, co. Carlow, **63**
Steelboys, 126
Stevens, John, 54
Strabane, 76, 80, 84, 129
Strikes, 151, 168
Sullivan, B., **88**
Swift, Jonathan, 116

Tamehager [Tomhaggard], co. Wexford, 45
Tara, 9, 14
Tavernere, Richard, 40
Taverns, 44, 68
Tea, 104, 111, 163–6, 171
Thackeray, William, 132, 133, 136, 137
Theatre, 68, 104, **106**
Tilting, **42**, 44
Tipperary, 95, 126
  co., 109, 128
Tithes, 94–5, 126
Tobacco, 52–3, 66
Tourism, tourists, 55, 75, 132
Towns, 9, 18, 20, 22, 23, 26–7, 28, 30, 35–9, 45, 48, 50, 65–6, 84–7, 129, 132, 148–51
Townswomen, **39**
Trade, 16–17, 18, 21, 27, 29–30, 38–9, 45, 48, 51, 52–3, 71–3, 156, 162–3, 167
Trade Unions, 168–9
Tramore, 109, 134
Trapping, 2, **3**, 4, 18

Travel, 9–10, 54–5, 75, 76–7, 132–3, 153–4
  see also Coaches and coaching, Stage-coaches and Railways
Trench, W. Steuart, 146
Trinity College, 96, 132
Tuath, 5, 9, 11, 12, 13, 17, 18, 22
Tullaghobegley, co. Donegal, 124, 158
Tullaghoge, **27**
Tullamore, 79
Turnpikes, 73–4
Turf, **77**, **91**, **116**
Twiss, Richard, 74, 75, 76, 77
Tyreragh, co. Sligo, 119
Tyrone, co., 103, 128

Ulster, 5, 23, 81, 82, 123, 128
United Irishmen, 127
Union, 91, 135
Unrest, agrarian, 126, 128, 145–6, 152–3
University, 48 see also Trinity College

Vandaleur estate, **153**
Vaughan, James, 73

Wages, 112–14, 119, 121, 122, 147, 159, 167, 168
Wakefield, Edward, 107
Wakes, 64
Walls, town, 20, 35, 38, 65–6, 85–6
Warfare, 14–15, 25, 28, 31, 55–6
Waring, Jane, **136**
Warrior, **13**, **14**
Water-supply, 37, **148**, 150, 169
Waterford, 30, **34**, 35, 37, 45, 76, 134
  co., 122
Waterways, 78–9
Weaving, 81–2, 125–6, 146
Westmeath, co., 120
Westport, 119
Wexford, 168
  co., 107, 124, 127, 144
Whiskey, 45, 64, 87
Whiteboys, 126
Wicklow, co., 144
  mountains, 129
Wine, 17, 22, 38, 45
Wolves, 6, 8, 50
Wool, 32, 72, 74
  spinning, 113
  spinning and weaving, 81
Woollen industry, 93
Workhouse, **141**

Youghal, 30, **53**
Young, Arthur, 74, 75, 77, 79, 80, 85, 87, 88, 98, 99, 102, 104, 106, 107, 109, 110, 111, 112, 115, 119, 120